THE GREAT
PATTERDALE TERRIER

JENNIFER & MICHAEL MILLER

THUNDERBOLT ISLAND
ATLANTA, GEORGIA

TheGreatPatterdaleTerrier@ThunderboltIsland.com

Jennifer & Michael Miller/Thunderbolt Island, LLC
www.TheGreatPatterdaleTerrier.com

Ordering Information:
Quantity sales. Special discounts are available on quantity purchases by corporations, associations, and others. For details, contact the "Special Sales Department" at the email address provided above.

Critique Partner: Catherine Miller
Cover Design by BespokeBookCovers.com

The Great Patterdale Terrier / Jennifer & Michael Miller —1st ed.
ISBN 978-0-9898652-0-3

Contents

To GOD, and his blessed gift of mental stability
And to our DOGs, that challenge its permanency

Figure 1: "A Likely Couple" ©, 2003. Painting by Vic Granger.

"The best gifts are found in furry packages."

THE MILLERS

Figure 2: "Voodoo", held by Skylar Miller.
Photograph taken in May 2010 in Atlanta, GA, USA.

Introduction

I FELL IN LOVE with the first stray that walked into my life. I was seven and he followed me home from the streets of North East Minneapolis. By the time we got back to my grandmother's house we were best friends. We spent the day wrestling and rolling around on the front lawn. My grandmother chased him out of the yard with a broom that evening. My dirty, ragtag buddy was back the next morning, waiting at the gate. I gave him a bath to make him more presentable. That night, my grandmother used a rake to shoo him away. I don't know if it was his freshly washed hair, his persistence, or her lack of lawn implements that softened her resolve, but on day three my grandmother told me she was too old to be running the dog off every night. I named him Boomerang, Boomer for short. That night Boomer slept in my room.

I fell in love with my wife even after she described herself as "more of a cat person". We moved into our home together with my canine son, a beautiful, loving American Pit Bull Terrier named Moses. After we settled in together, I suggested we make an addition to our family. The very next weekend we went to see a 4-month-old Jack Russell Terrier mix at a local rescue. My wife picked him up from his pen and gazed in his puppy eyes and fell in love. That night, Captain Morgan slept in our room.

Over the years, my wife and I have shared our rooms with canine companions of all shapes, sizes and pedigrees. We fell in love with them all. However, we have fallen under the spell of one extraordinary type of dog: the Patterdale Terrier. We love their indomitable spirit and drive. They have the ability to do seemingly everything well and a personality that keeps us laughing most of the day.

Another wonderful thing about these dogs is the people that are attached to them. Patterdale Terriers are relatively uncommon in the United States, so people involved with these dogs have gone out of their way to find them. This results in fascinating people passionate about their Patterdales and eager to share their stories. This book was written for people passionate about Patterdale Terriers: for present and future Patterdale followers who wish to get the most from their relationship with these remarkable dogs.

The purpose of this book is to provide a firm grounding in Patterdale Terriers for newly introduced admirers and seasoned connoisseurs alike. To accomplish this assignment it begins with a history of the Patterdale type to get a firm footing on their roots. Understanding their roots isn't essential for enjoying these delightful companions, but it sure does explain a lot about them. The book then delves into general Patterdale personality (albeit this is challenging because each Pat has his own identity). A chapter describes general characteristics and the breed standard by registry. Reflections are offered to help determine if a Patterdale Terrier would be a good match for your family and considerations for picking out your new best friend are included. There are chapters dedicated to the special needs of both puppies and mature dogs. The book walks you through the essentials of a good diet and how to design one for a healthy, happy dog. Grooming and healthcare subjects are covered along with first aid needs. Guidance on basic training is detailed. Wide-ranging information is delivered for fun activities like: Go-to-Ground, Racing, Flying Disc, Agility, Dock Jumping, and Obedience. This book shares tips on traveling and concludes with some wonderful story submissions from Patterdale devotees from around the world.

Putting this book together was filled with challenges for my wife and me. We are not professional writers but professional Patterdale Terrier enthusiasts. We have a renewed admiration for writers and the difficulties in getting a book published. In the end, we're glad we put it together because of the wonderful feedback we've received and the new friendships we've forged.

When we ask ourselves the question "why do dogs hold such a special place in our hearts?" The answer can be stated in two words: unconditional love. Our dogs only want to love us. They have no room in their hearts for judgment. They won't wake up one day and decide they need a change and move to another family. They don't care about material goods or grow jealous of the Pomeranian next door. Dogs are perfect. We have a lot to learn from them.

This book is written for dogs and the people that love them. We hope that reading this book brings you enjoyment and deepens the relationship you have with your furry colleague. Writing it certainly had that effect on our family.

—THE MILLERS
   Michael, Jennifer, Skylar, Blackened Voodoo, Sahara, Carrabelle, & Rio

Figure 3: Photograph used with permission by Chris Meagh.

"You have to know the past to understand the present."

Dr. Carl Sagan

Figure 4: "Cooling Off", featuring "Tarn" the Patterdale Terrier,
taken March, 2011 at Derwentwater in the
English Lake District, North West England.
Photograph used with permission by Jamie Green.

[1]

History of "The Little Black Dog"

I LET VOODOO OUT in the yard for his morning constitution while I brew my morning coffee. I need to prepare myself for the gray cubicle-habitrail existence that will imprison my attention for the next ten hours. Two seconds after I see the first drop of caffeine-laden elixir fall into my carafe, I hear faint but repetitive barks emanating from the backyard. Curious, I slip into my shoes and step from the air-cooled comfort of my home to the outdoor steam bath that saturates Atlanta in August. It's definitely Voodoo's tenacious spirit behind those yaps but where is he? The backyard is less than a half-acre fenced in, so there are not many places to hide. Is he under the deck? No. How about in the PVC tunnel activity center I built for him? No. I check the chipmunk hole he so graciously excavated the day before so it would more comfortably accommodate his ultra-assertive cranium. No, he's not there. No, the barking appears to be coming from the shed where we keep our lawn tools. I open the door and walk in. Still no Voodoo, but the sounds seem to be coming from the plywood floor. Sometimes I think that dog could find trouble in a four-by-four foot padded room (undoubtedly he would rip apart the cushioned walls because he felt they mocked him). I walk around the shed searching for a point of entry. I find a freshly dug hole maybe three inches high by six inches wide at the bottom of one of the outer walls. I drop to my knees and the barks grow louder. "Voodoo!" I yell forcefully and the bark skips a beat and then begins again. I would love to get a shovel and see what Voodoo has found this time but I have a morning meeting that I have to get to. Reluctantly I head back inside, finish my morning coffee ritual, and head to work.

I call Jen at lunchtime and she tells me that the barking persisted over the next two hours until she saw a cat run over the fence, Voodoo hot on its tail. When I let him out later that day I follow him over to his new hole, curious as to how he was able to enter such a small space. He sniffs the hole and crawls in on his side using his legs as leverage. He reappears a few minutes later with a thick dusting of dirt and a big white grin. I can't hold back the laughter.

PATTERDALE TERRIER HISTORY 101

I know how much we all loved history in high school, but the story of the Patterdale Terrier is worth a thoughtful read. As breeding programs go, Patterdales are certainly a newer type having only been labeled in the 1920's. To truly understand the dog we must understand his birthplace, the environment, its people, and the work he is needed to do.

The Lake District is an area on the Northwest coast of England, which borders Scotland. It could most easily be described as a country of contrasts: fused of rock, water, and wind. It is a hard land of rocky soil. Its landscape is covered with bare stone mountains (known as fells), rivers, and lakes.

Figure 5: "2008 Lake District – Langdale Pikes", photograph by Thierry Gregorius.
This work is licensed under a Creative Commons Attribution 3.0 United States License.

If the rugged terrain wasn't enough, the climate here is unforgiving. A damp mist covers much of the land for days on end. It is the wettest region of England with a precipitation of more than 80 inches annually. Patterdale, the city itself, is in a valley of the Lake District which typically exhibits 20 days of falling snow, 200 days of rain, and 145 dry days a year. Because of its location on the coast, the Lake District is very windy, particularly in the Fells, and due to the seemingly ever-present mist this territory averages only 2.5 hours of sunshine a day.

This is a very harsh environment unsuitable for sustainable agriculture. Its hilly topography is too rugged for cattle. It is for these reasons that this rural area has turned to sheep farming for its dominant trade. These are hard-working people toiling in isolated remote areas.

As difficult as a shepherd's life is, in this region their livelihood is often subject to predation by the indigenous foxes of the area. Any fox believed to have taken to killing sheep becomes an enemy of the hardworking shepherds and terrier men are enlisted to find such foxes and dispatch them. In the south of England where the land is soft, terrier men often travel on horseback. Here terriers are bred to bolt a fox from his hole or bay and hold him until humans can dig to him. In these areas we see dogs typified by the Jack Russell Terrier.

In the hard and rocky fells of the Northwest England Lake District, the huntsman is more limited in his options. Horses cannot be used, as the land is too rocky. This leads the terrier man and his terrier to cover miles of craggy mountainside on foot each day. Likewise digging to quarry in this inhospitable habitat is often not viable. Here terriers are bred to bolt fox or dispatch them underground if they choose to stand and fight. These terriers are known as Fell Terriers for the area in which they are bred and hunt and have passed their genes down from generation to generation for centuries. They are tough enough to cover many hard miles each day and still go to ground against a most formidable quarry and dispatch it when necessary. It is this land where our Patterdale Terriers began; forged from a hard land, harsh conditions, and a strong people.

In 1873, two hunt packs (the Patterdale and the Matterdale) were joined to create the Ullswater Foxhounds. In 1879, Joe Bowman began hunting this pack. Joe Bowman hunted the Ullswater hounds from 1879 to 1924. He became one of the most celebrated huntsmen of England and was even memorialized in song:

> *When the fire's on the hearth and good cheer abounds,*
> *We'll drink to Joe Bowman and his Ullswater hounds,*
> *For we ne'er shall forget how he woke us at dawn*
> *With the crack of his whip and the sound of his horn. (Black, 2011)*

Joe was a Border Terrier breeder and it is from his program that he named the first Patterdale Terrier. Joe crossed a blue-black Border Terrier with a black-and-tan Fell Terrier (also known as the working Lakeland Terrier) to start the beginnings of the Patterdale Terrier type. Interestingly, Joe was born in the small village of Patterdale that lies in a valley just south of Ullswater, which supposedly contributed to his choice of names. Joe Bowman is the progenitor of our Patterdale Terrier and we know it began to be known as a type within the Ullswater Foxhounds by the 1920s. Joe Bowman lived until 1940 when he died at the age of 90.

Figure 6: "Martini", taken January, 2010 at
Monmouth Battlefield State Park, Manalapan, NJ, USA.
Photograph used with permission by Chris Miller.

Our Patterdale Terrier history now turns its attention 60 miles east of Ullswater to Middleham. It was here in the 1930s that Cyril Breay met Frank Buck and the future of the Patterdale Terrier would be spawned. Cyril was a knowledgeable breeder who began with Sealyham Terriers but soon turned his attention toward Fell Terriers without crossings to Border Terrier blood. Cyril was a "gameness" zealot and Frank became a partner in that pursuit. "Gameness" is a term coined by the dog community to describe the unstoppable drive and determination of a few revered animals. Dogs described as "game" don't understand the meaning of the word quit and never back down from their goal regardless of personal pain, injury, or fear. Buck and Breay only bred the gamest animals together to produce a strain highly sought after by terrier men of the area. They tested their stock on badger, mink, and fox. Frank Buck did terrier work for the Bedale Foxhounds, the Wesleydale Harriers, and the West of Yore Hound Pack. He was a well-respected and tireless worker and his dogs earned the same reputation.

It has been said Frank Buck introduced some of Joe Bowman's stock to their line, which explains the connection to the Patterdale name. Regardless of the validity of that explanation, the strain bred by Cyril and Frank became what we now know as the Patterdale Terrier. Their breeding program of only breeding the gamest dogs together began to typify in the 1950s and they continued their strain into the 1970s when Cyril Breay died.

As Joe Bowman is known as the progenitor of the Patterdale Terrier and Cyril Breay with Frank Buck are known as the originators of the type, Brian Nuttall has become the caretaker and ambassador introducing Pats to the world. Brian's father moved with Cyril Breay north to Mallerstang from the South of Wales, each of them bringing their Sealyham Terriers with them. Cyril was very attracted to badger hunting, which the Sealyhams were bred for, but found the breed less than ideal for this northern terrain. It was for this reason he began breeding the Fell Terriers more aggressively and built out the Patterdale Terrier line.

Brian Nuttall had the opportunity to hunt with both Cyril Breay and Frank Buck and soon began breeding his family's line of terriers to those of Buck and Breay in the 1950s. Brian was like Cyril, a very strict breeder and would not breed to any dog until it had proven game to fox. It is interesting to note that while the dogs bred by Cyril's hand tended to favor red-coated terriers, Brian tended to turn more toward smooth coated black terriers. It could also be mentioned that Cyril Breay's dogs fluctuated much more in size reaching as much as 16 inches at the shoulder where Nuttall's dogs stay more in the 10 to 12 inch range suitable for fox hunting in the region.

While there is no doubt of the influence of Breay and Buck ancestry in Nuttall's strain, Brian has been credited with fixing the type. In the time in which this book has been written, almost any Patterdale Terrier found is within seven degrees of separation from Brian Nuttall's stock. He is a revered and prolific breeder of Patterdales. Brian Nuttall sent the first Patterdale to the United States in 1978. In 1993, the Patterdale Terrier Club of America (PTCA) was founded and the Patterdale Terrier was finally recognized as a breed. The United Kennel Club (UKC) followed suit with their recognition in 1995.

The history of the Patterdale Terrier is scattered and rough, much like the cold and rainy mountains from whence he was forged. Greater detail of the land and the people and stories of early cornerstone dogs can be found in Sean Frain's *Patterdale Terrier* (Frain, 2004) or D. Brian Plummer's *The Fell Terrier* (Plummer, 1998). Both are great historical works and are listed in the Bibliography as resources.

Figure 7: "The Cragged Fox" ©, 2006. Painting by Vic Granger.

"A quiet personality sure isn't what you need to attract attention."

Bill Budge

Figure 8: "Henry, Bohdi, and Ollie", taken April 2014
at Reiss Beach, Caithness in Scottish Highlands, Scotland.
Photograph used with permission by Kirsty Moore.

[2]

Patterdale Personality

JEN AND I really enjoy getting our hands dirty and greens keeping. We are often complimented on our front yard from passersby. These people appreciate the time and effort we put into landscaping and enjoy the beauty of our lush lawn and the flowering accouterments we've nurtured over the years. It always brings a smirk to our faces when people make kind comments about our green space. We're sure their tone would change if they wandered into the war-torn minefield that is our backyard. This part of the property falls under the care of our canine companions. They too have a knack for greens keeping. Their agronomic policy follows one golden rule: "If an intruding animal makes a hole in our yard, then we need to make it bigger!" Voodoo is a particularly fervent devotee of this rule. When he was just four months old he was working on a new chipmunk entrance with Carrabelle, his adoptive Jack Russell sister. They were determined to find their way into this entry no matter how long or how much effort it would take. At one point they dug enough for Voodoo to fit his full head into the opening. Unfortunately his shoulders kept him from going any further. For a moment his body, with little legs still kicking, was straight up in the air. He looked like he was doing a headstand without the benefit of his head. Patterdales amaze and amuse us with their determination; especially when the task they are attempting defies the laws of physics or gravity.

PERSONALITY PLUS

Talk to anyone who's been around Pats and there is one statement that will be asserted without challenge, "Patterdale Terriers have personality plus". It is principal to understand where this personality is rooted. It is seeded from the fells; germinated from

9

a cold, rocky, rainy environment; sprouted from a demanding, exhaustive, and often perilous profession; and shaped by a people with an extreme work ethic, intolerant of anything less from their dogs.

There are three pillars to your Patterdale Terrier's personality and foremost among them is his work comes first. There is nothing more important to your companion than his job. He will work without fear and little regard to his personal well-being to accomplish the task at hand. Whether his job is to go underground and excavate a fierce fox from its den or return a tennis ball launched into the yard over and over again, he is serious about success. Understanding this determination, this need for a job, it is important for you to assign him one. Pats who are not given an occupation will find one on their own, and chances are you won't be happy with the one of his choosing. Teach him how to fetch and make time for his job every day, or teach him nothing and let him decide to chew on the legs of your dining room table day after day.

The second thing you need to know about your canine friend is his need for exercise. Once again this comes from his work, climbing the fells for hours a day without rest. Make sure he gets his daily allotment of exercise, or once again his positive energy may manifest itself into a destructive habit.

Finally, it is important to understand your Patterdale Terrier's confidence. This is probably the greatest trait that can be bestowed on a dog but does come with great responsibility. Many people confuse confidence or fearlessness with aggression. Nothing could be further from the truth; most dog attacks on people are a direct result of fear in dogs. Dogs that are fearful are unpredictable and unreliable in uncomfortable situations. Dogs that are confident have little fear and behave as expected. To cultivate that confidence and teach your friend appropriate behavior, Patterdales need to be exposed to a variety of different stimuli in controlled, non-frightening conditions, particularly while they're young. Exposing your friend to different situations will increase his confidence and enforce what expected manners are in any circumstance.

Patterdale Terriers are hardworking, energetic, confident dogs. They thrive on strong, active, dependable relationships with their humans. How do you know if one of these lively little guys is the right fit for you? Questions to ask include: Are you ready to make a 15-year commitment? Patterdale Terriers live an average of 11 to 13 years but some have lived to be 16 years or even older. Do you travel a lot? If you travel frequently and would need to kennel your furry friend regularly, please don't get a Patterdale. They thrive on companionship and should not spend days sequestered alone. After an average day at work are you content to lie on the sofa and watch TV? Pats love a little couch cuddle time but they also need their daily exercise.

While Patterdale Terriers get along with all personality types, an ideal human companion would be someone who is active and enjoys the outdoors. Pats match well with people who have active lifestyles. Are you a runner or take long hikes? These spunky little guys are always ready to go. If you are someone with a low energy level, it might be best to look at another dog breed. We are fortunate that Jen is a distance runner and Voodoo is her favorite companion, often the two will put in 12 miles of running in a day. Patterdales love to be outside, and love getting dirty. Is there something dead and smelly in the backyard? The first thing he'll do is flop to his back and cover himself with this horribly objectionable new scent.

Figure 9: "Candy", taken in April 2014 in Ruskin, FL, USA.
Photograph used with permission by Anglo-American Patterdales.

These active terriers need fresh air and room to move. Apartments are not the ideal living spaces, although they will suit your Patterdale fine if he gets adequate exercise. If you have a yard that is big enough for him to run around and dig, you would be a good match for a Patterdale. If you do not have a backyard, plan on making a commitment to taking several trips to the park (preferably a dog park if one is available to you) each week. You will need at least one good walk per day as well. On rainy days, an option for his exercise need is to work your dog on a treadmill. If you are considering bringing a Patterdale home but lack the adequate amount of time and space to dedicate to this dog, you would be advised against doing so for both the dog's sake and your own.

Patterdales love to dig, so be prepared for a few backyard holes here and there. Another thing to worry about is your determined little Pat digging under the fence and escaping to chase a squirrel taunting him on the other side. If you have holes in your backyard from chipmunks or other underground-dwellers, expect that your Patterdale will sniff them out and excavate them. Prepare yourself for the occasional cadavers of small mammals to mysteriously appear on your deck.

Outdoors, a Patterdale should always be kept on a lead or inside a secure area, as they will chase after anything that moves. It is their natural instinct to chase and hunt. In the event that they are able to escape, it can be very difficult to catch or call them back once their mind locks on to something. If you are not someone who is capable of chasing after a loose dog, whether by age or physical ability, then a Patterdale might not be the best match for you. Patterdales are quick and curious, so always make sure you have a firm grip of their lead as their focus will wander to any bird or small creature and it can be difficult to divert their attention back to your walk.

By nature, the Patterdale Terrier is a very alert and determined hunter. They crave the hunt and have an ingrained prey drive. When on the chase, these small dogs are surprisingly quick, and pose a threat to all small woodland creatures in their path. You may be surprised to learn that your Patterdale is not overly selective in distinguishing what is prey and what isn't. If your home has a small pet like a hamster or rabbit - it may not for long. Once the dog sees a bolting bundle of fur, the chase is on. Cats and other animals should also be supervised in the company of Patterdale Terriers, due to the dogs' natural hunting instinct. Your Patterdale Terrier is very aware of his surroundings and usually serves as an effective watchdog by announcing the arrival of guests and potentially unwanted visitors.

The Patterdale Terrier is a tough little individual bred to hike the fells for miles and still have the stamina to go down and challenge foxes in their dens. The Patterdale Terrier is a big dog in a small package. Patterdales are known to take on challenges that are too large for them and therefore require a great deal of supervision. But with proper direction, Patterdale Terriers are wonderful family pets particularly in homes with active adults or children to play with. They really get along with everyone and are not the classic one-person dog some other breeds are known to produce.

Pats have pleasant and cheerful personalities. They are content to curl up with you, or go to work chasing varmints. Having gained the reputation of being tough, excellent hunters they have also proven to possess the traits of an ideal companion. They work hard and play hard. Their immense stamina allows the dog to hunt all day and still be a lively playmate of children when they come home from school. When properly trained, your Pat will offer you unquestionable loyalty. When socialized from a young age, Patterdale Terriers get along well with small children and other pets, often making friends quickly. Keep them exercised and occupied with tasks, and they'll mature to be happy companions.

If you are planning to have a Patterdale as a family pet, it is important to socialize him when he is a puppy. From very early on, have your children play with your puppy. Children love to carry puppies around and should be encouraged as long as they are old enough to be respectful, kind, and not scare the pup. Having your children around the puppy from an early age will ensure that your Patterdale will grow into an adult dog that will be friendly to other children. If you do not have children around, it is important to make sure that the puppy becomes familiar with people and the world around them. Take your Patterdale to public places where there are plenty of people around. Parks are ideal spots for socialization.

Patterdale Terriers are supremely confident. They do not need constant attention and affirmations. This is not to say that they do not appreciate attention, because they certainly do. You will often times find your Patterdale off sitting by himself, resting in a corner, or gazing out at the yard peacefully. Unlike many non-working dogs, they do not need to be constantly held and are not lap dogs. They do not need to be at your side at all times. They are working dogs, which are content with themselves and with other dogs. This is not to say that they do not enjoy sitting on your lap during their down time. They are very loving dogs, and enjoy being close by your side when they are resting.

Figure 10: "Penny" and "Bond", taken June 2014 at
the Bure River in Buxton, Norfolk, UK.
Photograph used with permission by Craig Trussell.

Patterdales can do well with other dogs and are commonly used in packs while hunting. A hunter usually takes two to four of these dogs to hunt. Thus, a Patterdale Terrier can become accustomed to working with other dogs. They have a pack mentality seeded from their history of going out in groups to hunt. If you already have dogs at home, your new Patterdale Terrier will probably fit in just fine. But given the choice it is always wiser to avoid same sex canine partners. If you end up with two alpha dogs of the same gender, the battles can be vicious. If you do not have other dogs, dog parks are great places for your dog to meet other dogs and get used to seeing them. If you have local dog shows in your area, you could take them there to meet other dogs. If you plan on showing your Patterdale, this would be an ideal way to get them used to the environment as well. Teaching your Patterdale to tolerate the presence of other dogs without turning aggressive is an important development in their personality. If you are unsure where to socialize your dog, you could check online for meet up groups or with your veterinarian to see if she knows of any social clubs you can join.

Patterdales are very intelligent. They respond quickly to training, as they are eager to please their owner. A willing learner, the Patterdale Terrier generally responds well to basic training and commands. These bright dogs have the ability to learn to perform most any task their trainer is willing to take the time to teach. Establishing immediate dominance, trust, and respect is the key to successfully training the Patterdale Terrier. This breed responds best to a confident and caring handler with a stern yet gentle approach to repetitive exercises and tasks. Patterdales, while having strong personalities, are also sensitive creatures. It is important when training them to be strong, but not overbearing. This could make them shy and lower their confidence. Praise them strongly, and correct them when they are wrong. The goal of Patterdale training is to shape them into well-behaved and trustworthy canines.

Patterdales are full of life and curiosity. It is this curiosity that often times leads to mischief when they are not properly supervised. Pats who do not receive the right amount of exercise and space will often act out by destroying things. They will use their genetic traits in negative ways, by chewing, digging, barking, and ignoring basic training like housebreaking in order to release their energy. Patterdales are not couch potatoes. If they are not adequately exercised they will become bored which will lead to destructive behavior. Be prepared to work a long walk in every day if you do not have a yard. Don't forget to allow for a little playtime at home with their favorite chew toy as well.

Although Patterdale Terriers are a working breed, they can be brought up as excellent family pets. Their versatile personality is one of their most interesting traits. Make sure that you have given this chapter thought before taking home a Patterdale. The Patterdale Terrier is energetic and determined with the ability to be obedient, loyal, and affectionate. They make fantastic hunting dogs, family pets, and companions alike.

"Why not be oneself? That is the whole secret of a successful appearance. If one is a Greyhound, why try to look like a Pekingese?"

Dame Edith Sitwell

Figure 11: "Beag", taken March 2014 in the
Kerry Mountains, County Kerry, Ireland.
Photograph used with permission by Liam O Shea.

[3]

Appearance & Standards

CAPTAIN MORGAN WAS an obsessive ball freak from the very beginning. He never grew tired of playing fetch and we played with him nearly every day. We would stand on the deck, launching the ball over and over into the backyard. Every time he would find it and bring it back dropping just out of hands reach and pushing it to us with his nose. He didn't want to put it in our hand, as that would indicate he was trained to fetch. Instead, he trained us to bend down, pick it up and throw it for him. He was exceptionally proficient at finding the ball no matter where it landed. Over time we made it more and more difficult, throwing the ball into a patch of ivy or deep in a pile of leaves, requiring him to use his nose to sniff it out.

My husband and I are true beach spirits. There is nothing we enjoy quite as much as walking along a shoreline, enjoying the sound of the surf, the sand in our toes and the serenity that washes over us. We were thrilled when we found a beach on the coast that allowed dogs. One day on a beach walk I began throwing a ball a little in front of us on the beach so Captain could run up ahead and grab it and bring it back. By accident, I threw a wayward lob and it landed in the surf. Without missing a beat Captain tracked the ball into the surf and returned it. "Well this was interesting", I thought. "Would Captain swim for a ball?" Captain had never shown much interest in swimming to this point. The tide was very calm that day, so I threw a ball a little ways out in the water. Sure enough Captain tracked it and swam out to the ball and brought it back. This was fun, now every ball I threw was into the ocean and they started going further and further out, testing his resolve. Every time Captain found it and returned it. I loved the tenacious spirit of that little terrier.

The next day I took Captain by myself to the beach. I let him off the lead and he ran straight to the surf waiting expectantly for me to throw the ball into the ocean.

The choppy waves on that day concerned me. So I threw a little toss, and he quickly returned it, dropping it at my feet, begging me for something more challenging. So I threw it into the surf, preparing myself to jump in after him. Captain vaulted himself into the waves. His head came up 3 seconds later just past where the waves were breaking. He started scanning left and right for the ball. When he found it he swam after it and body surfed his way back to the beach. He dropped the ball at my feet and spit up a tummy-full of saltwater. Then he began pushing the ball at me to play again.

Captain began to love ocean fetch. It was his favorite game. He learned how to time a crashing wave so he could leap just as it was falling. Planning to swim out before the next one came in. He was fearless, tireless, and absolutely remarkable. People would stop and watch us, amazed at his ability and concerned for his safety. They saw similar fetching on the beach from the retrievers that visited the area, but never from a dog so tiny. To this day, every time my family goes on the beach we think of that little terrier and recall stories of his awe-inspiring determination.

Form Follows Function

People who saw him were amazed at Captain's swimming and fetching ability. Why were they amazed? It wasn't that they hadn't seen such ability from the local Labrador and Golden Retrievers that frequented the beach. It was that they had never seen this strength, determination and skill in such a small form. Now honestly, regardless of how good a retriever Captain was in the ocean, he would never be able to fetch a ball as quickly as a capable Labrador or Golden Retriever. These canines have the correct form for fetching. They are bigger and better equipped to handle large waves. But the most important trait was Captain's never-quit attitude and how well he performed his "function" regardless of his "form".

Showing your Patterdale can be a lot of fun, particularly when you understand that the most important trait of this terrier is his function. All other characteristics and standards for judging stem from his functionality and what he is bred to do; which is hunt underground. How does his appearance affect the way he will work? This is how a Patterdale Terrier is judged at a dog show. Keep in mind that form follows function.

There are appearance generalities we can apply to our Patterdale friend. There are physical traits that allow him to do his job well. How will we know how good he is at bolting quarry from its den if he's too large and barrel-chested to fit down the foxhole? A dog too large to go-to-ground may be a wonderful household companion, agility champion, or even barn hunter; but he should not be bred as a Patterdale Terrier. These quintessential terriers were bred for their accomplishments in the field. In their genes course incredible drive, spirit, and the physical traits necessary to be amazing go-to-ground hunters.

One of the wonderful characteristics of these indomitable little guys is their individuality. Look at their coats: rough, broken, smooth - all textures are welcome. Why? Because none of these coat varieties affect how good a worker he will be. We are fortunate Patterdale Terriers have not claimed "breed" status. They have yet to be recognized by the largest kennel clubs (i.e. the Kennel Club of the United Kingdom and the American Kennel Club of the United States). These breed registries spend a large focus on a dog's looks. Take for example the Westminster Dog Show, the most publicized dog pageant in the world. Look at the terrier contestants. I would be surprised if one of these animals knew what dirt looked like, much less how to work it. Yet there they are paraded before the world as the apex examples of their respective breeds. Winning dogs of these fashion shows are then bred with preference and slowly destroy a working dog breed until it is little more a caricature of its former self. We should consider ourselves fortunate that our little dog is as of yet only recognized by working dog clubs focused more on the abilities of the dogs rather than their appearance.

In England where he was formed, the Patterdale Terrier is considered a "type" and not a "breed". The critical distinction being that a "type" follows the philosophy of only breeding working stock to working stock. As of the year of this publishing (2014) there are a few major clubs that publish a breed standard for our Pats, the two largest being: the Patterdale Terrier Club of America (PTCA) and the United Kennel Club (UKC). Their forgiving breed standards are reprinted with their permission as follows:

Figure 12: "Dusty", "Sweep", and "Sooty". Photograph used with permission by Ma Wood.

PATTERDALE TERRIER CLUB OF AMERICA (PTCA)

GENERAL APPEARANCE

- The Patterdale Terrier is a tough, active terrier and should give a compact, well-balanced image.
- Height should be between 10" to 15" measured at the shoulders.
- Weight should be proportionate, presenting neither a "weedy" or "clunky" image.

CHEST

- As a working terrier, the Patterdale must be able to follow its quarry through small tunnels. If the chest is too big, the terrier will not be able to complete its job efficiently. As a general rule, you should be able to "hand span" the terrier's chest with the fingers of both hands touching.

BACK

- The back should be strong and level, with length in proportion to the dog's height. If the back is too short the terrier may not be flexible enough to move around underground.

LEGS

- The legs should be straight, with good bone, the feet turning neither in nor out.
- The rear should have good angulation, with the hocks turning neither in nor out.

HEAD AND MUZZLE

- The head should give the impression of strength and be in proportion to the rest of the body.
- The muzzle should not appear snippy or too blocky.

TEETH

- The teeth should meet in a scissors bite; however a level bite is acceptable.
- Undershot or overshot is a fault, and should be considered in the working context.
- Teeth lost or broken while working will not be penalized.

EARS

- Button ear, with tight fold, and tips of ears meeting the skull at the corner of the eye.

NECK

- The neck should be muscular and proportionate to the head and body.

TAIL

- The tail should be set high on rump.
- It should not be carried over the back.
- If you choose to dock, no more than 1/4 should be removed.
- As an adult, approximately a "palm's width" is preferable, should provide a good "hand-hold".

Coat

- The coat may be "Smooth", "Broken" or "Rough".
- All types should be dense and coarse.
- Smooth: coarse, overall very short, smooth
- Broken: coarse, longer hair on body except for head and ears, which is smooth. Maybe some longer whiskering on muzzle and chin.
- Rough: coarse, longer hair overall, including face and ears

Color

- Colors include: Black, Red, Chocolate, or Black and Tan
- (There may be some variations in the primary colors. For instance, blacks may have some lighter hairs, red may range from tan to deep rust, chocolate may be a very dark chestnut, or lighter brown (a true chocolate will have a brown/red nose) and black and tan may have more or less of these colors on each individual dog, but the only registerable colors are those listed above)
- Chocolate-colored dogs will have a brown nose. (Officially called a "red" nose)
- Some white on chest and feet is acceptable.

Height and Weight

- Height may range from 10 to 15 inches.
- Weight should be proportionate to the terrier's height.
- A very muscular dog will weigh more than it looks.
- You should be able to feel the ribs, but not see them.

Disqualifications

- (1) Cryptorchid - one or both testicles fail to descend into the scrotum
- (2) Shyness or viciousness
- Terriers with these disqualifications should not be bred.

Note

- Used by permission of Robert Burns, ©Copyright Robert Burns 1993.

Figure 13: "Wilbur" is an example of a "red" Patterdale Terrier.
Photo taken in 2009 at Simmons Park in Ruskin, FL, USA,
Photograph used with permission by Anglo-American Patterdales.

UNITED KENNEL CLUB (UKC)

GENERAL APPEARANCE

- The A sturdy, tough, active little terrier that presents a compact, balanced image. As a working terrier, it has to be capable of squeezing through very small passages underground to follow its quarry. The Patterdale's chest should be capable of being spanned behind the shoulders by an average man's hands with the fingers of both hands touching.
- Patterdales stand between 10 and 15 inches tall at the withers (part of the dog between the back, the neck and the shoulders).
- This breed is worked far more than it is shown, and breeders are primarily concerned with the practicality of the breed. This terrier must have a strong neck, powerful jaws and teeth, the fortitude to hold its quarry at bay, and the

ability to squeeze into tight burrows. He must have great flexibility and endurance.

- Scars resulting from wounds received while working are considered honorable and are not to be penalized.

CHARACTERISTICS

- The Patterdale is an extremely courageous working terrier, traditionally used to go to ground. Patterdales are extremely willing to work and have a high desire to please. They are very active and have a strong prey drive; and though they should be peaceful with humans, livestock and other dogs, they are not a dog for the average pet owner. They require an owner with a sense of humor and one that understands and can tolerate a real terrier temperament.

HEAD

- The head is strong and powerful, in balance with the size of the dog, and wedge or trapezoidal shaped when viewed from the front. The length of the skull and the muzzle are equal, or with the muzzle slightly shorter than the skull. Jowl and muzzle have good substance. The muzzle should be strong, never appearing snipy or weak.

TEETH

- A full complement of strong, white teeth meet in a scissor or level bite. Teeth that are broken, or incisors that are lost, due to working, are not to be penalized.

EYES

- The eyes are set squarely in the skull and fairly wide apart. As an earth-working terrier, it is important that the eyes not protrude or bulge. Eye color should be in harmony with the coat color, but never blue.

EARS

- The ears are triangular in shape, and small to moderate in size, folding tightly just above the skull. The tips point to the outside corner of the eye.

NOSE

- Black except in the liver-colored dogs, which have a red nose.

NECK

- The neck is clean, muscular and of moderate length, widening gradually from the nape and blending smoothly into the shoulders.
- Faults: Ewe-neck, neck too short or too thick.

FOREQUARTERS

- The shoulder is long, sloping and well laid back.

FORELEGS

- The shoulder is long, sloping and well laid back.
- Faults: Bowed legs; fiddle front; down in pasterns; toes turned out; knuckling over or any other misalignment of joints; out at the elbow.

BODY

- In proportion, the body should be square or slightly longer than tall, measured from the point of the shoulder to the point of the buttocks, and from the withers to the ground. The back is of moderate length and level, blending into a muscular, slightly arched loin that has slight to moderate tuck up.
- The chest should be firm yet flexible, deep to the level of the elbow but moderate in width and oval in shape.

SPANNING

- Spanning is an important part of the judging process for the Patterdale Terrier. They must be spanned to test for size, compression and flexibility. The Patterdale should be capable of being spanned directly behind the shoulders by an average sized mans hands. When spanning, lift the front legs off the ground or table and gently squeeze the bottom of the chest to be certain that the chest will compress.
- Faults: Chest too deep or wide, incapable of being spanned or lacking the ability to compress. Body too cobby or barrel shaped, causing lack of flexibility of the back.

Figure 14: Judge Lyn Harber spans a Patterdale at
the Gold Coast Terrier Network Trial,
February 2012 in Bronson, FL, USA.

HINDQUARTERS

- The hindquarters are strong and muscular. Bone, angulation and musculature match that of the forequarters.

HIND LEGS

- The stifles are well bent and the hocks are well let down. When the dog is standing, the short, strong rear pasterns are perpendicular to the ground, and when viewed from the rear they are parallel to one another.

TAIL

- The tail is set high but not carried over the back. If docked, only one-quarter to one-third should be removed, as sometimes the tail is the only means of pulling the dog out of a burrow. The tail should be strong but not overly thick. There is no preference between docked or natural.
- Serious Fault: Gay tail, carried forward over the back.

- Disqualification: Bobtail.

COAT

- The coat may be smooth or broken. In both coat types, there should be a short, dense undercoat. Very little grooming is required to keep the coat healthy.
- Smooth - hair is coarse, dense and stiff, falling back in place when lifted. No wave is present.
- Broken - an intermediate coat, having longer guard hairs than the smooth coat. The guard hairs are coarse and wiry and may be wavy. A broken coated dog may or may not have face furnishings that form a beard, moustache and eyebrows.
- A correct coat is important for protection against the wet underground and briars. Dogs with damaged coat sections that are due to hunting scars or abrasions should not be penalized in the show ring as long as overall texture can be determined.
- Serious Fault: Coat in any climate that is soft, long or downy in texture.

Figure 15: "Ozzy" is an example of a Patterdale with a broken coat.
Photo taken August 2012 in Dawlish, UK.
Photograph used with permission by Alan Dunnett.

COLOR

- Acceptable colors include black, red, liver, grizzle, black and tan, and bronze, either solid or with some white markings on chest and feet.
- Disqualification: Any patch or spot of white marking on the body or head. Not to be confused with scarring, which can cause white hairs to grow in.

HEIGHT & WEIGHT

- The Patterdale Terrier ranges in height from 10 to 15 inches at the withers. Weight should be in proportion to height, with dogs always shown in hard, fit, working condition with no excess fat.

GAIT

- When trotting, the gait is effortless, smooth, powerful, and well-coordinated, showing good but not exaggerated reach and drive. The topline remains level, with only a slight flexing to indicate suppleness. Viewed from any position, legs turn neither in nor out, nor do feet cross or interfere with each other. As speed increases, feet tend to converge toward centerline of balance.
- Movement faults should be penalized to the exent that they would interfere with the terrier's ability to work efficiently.

DISQUALIFICATIONS

- Unilateral or bilateral cryptorchid. Viciousness or extreme shyness. Albinism. Bob tail. Any patch or spot of white marking on the body or head. (Not to be confused with scarring, which can cause white hairs to grow in.)

NOTE

- This information has been contributed by, and is property of The United Kennel Club, and is gratefully used here with permission.

Patterdale terriers' appearance and standards should be judged solely on how that particular trait will affect their ability to do their job. The job of the Patterdale is to work the quarry, and the best looking dog might not always be the best working dog and vice versa. It is interesting to note how no penalties are to be made towards scarring, missing or broken teeth. It is considered to be a normal occurrence for a Patterdale to be working and having acquired such visual imperfections as a result of being a hard worker. This is yet another example of how Patterdales are such a unique and interesting breed. We need to end this chapter by stating that how your Patterdale Terrier places in dog shows should not be of great consequence to you. We would rather have a Patterdale that worked like the dickens with a spot of white fur on his head than a lesser worker that met the written standard.

Figure 16; "Alf" is a black and tan Patterdale Terrier.
Photo taken June 2011 in Darlington, UK.
Photograph used with permission by Ian Yarrow.

"We long for an affection altogether ignorant of our faults. Heaven has accorded this to us in the uncritical canine attachment."

George Eliot

Figure 17: "Voodoo", 6 months old.
Photograph taken in Atlanta, GA, June 2010.

[4]

Your Next Best Friend

MY MIND OFTEN WANDERS to a wet, windy day in the month of June. My husband, daughter, two canine sons and I were travelling through the Florida panhandle and needed a place to stretch our legs after seven hours cooped up in the car. We found respite in a small coastal town with a pet-friendly motel and the world's smallest police station - which certainly deserved a closer look. After taking in the diminutive site, we found a funky oyster shack for a bite to eat. While we were consuming our meal and discussing our travels, my husband pointed to a small terrier in the parking lot that reminded him of our dog Captain. I looked over and saw it had a little sibling as company and grinned at the sight of them. No sooner had the smile surfaced on my face then it was replaced with a ghostly white shadow. I jumped from my seat as an 18-wheeler nearly ran over one of the pups as they crossed the coastal highway. My husband read the panic on my face and simply said, "Go get them". I jumped from my seat and ran out the door as he called for the check.

I followed the scared pups, trying to block them from wandering onto the highway. The puppies were much younger than I had first thought; they were tiny with clumsy gaits. We played chase in a church parking lot momentarily and one sweet puppy jumped into my arms. My husband pulled up in our car with the rest of the family. I thrust this little girl into his arms and took off in the direction I last saw the other. I ran into what looked like a forgotten child's play yard. There was a green-water baby pool with a doll floating face down. There were what appeared to be dirty diapers scattered around the property. At this point, I spotted the second puppy climbing onto a dilapidated porch surrounded by torn screens. I tried my best to get that second puppy regardless of the fact I may have been trespassing. It disappeared a few minutes later and I couldn't find where it had gone. After another twenty minutes of searching without any luck, I sauntered back to the car and slid into the passenger seat. My daughter handed me the dog I had saved. I looked down at this flea-covered, worm-distended (round & tape), cherry-eyed dog and knew three things: first, this dog was going to take a lot of money to fix up; second, this dog was now officially a "Miller"; and third, her name would be Carrabelle for the town where we found her.

Are You Ready To Be A Patterdale Parent?

Let's talk about choices. Our days are filled with them, big and small. The small choices usually have little effect on our lives going forward. "Should I order the chopped chef salad or the spinach salad with balsamic vinaigrette?" Other decisions we make have long lasting implications. "Should I take that job offer in Katmandu?" This chapter is about dog choices.

The first doggie decision is the biggest one. "Should I share my life with a new dog?" When we chose to adopt Carrabelle from the road, it was a conscience decision. We didn't have to. We could have brought her to a rescue organization or never picked her up in the first place. When we made the decision to keep her, it was a big one. Looking back on it now if we hadn't chosen to adopt her, we wouldn't have holes in our sofa cushions or stains on our living room carpet. Of course we also wouldn't have a dog that has become our daughter's best friend, her partner in junior handling competitions and her bedtime snuggle buddy.

A new animal will rely on you for all aspects of its survival, from nutritional and shelter requirements to a need for attention and demands of your time. So before you bring that rambunctious canine home ask yourself some questions - and be honest with your answers.

Why do you want a dog?

That's a tough one, and there's no right answer. But we would hope that your choice isn't an impulsive one. It's hard to sustain a healthy long-term relationship spawned from a five-minute hasty decision. We all know how cute that little doggie in the window is (we would hope you aren't even considering buying a dog from a pet store), but it's easy to see that's not the best of reasons for getting a dog. Another case fraught with failure is getting a dog at your child's request. Your child is not equipped to make that choice for your family no matter how much she says she'll walk the dog and take care of it. It will still be your responsibility. Furthermore, it will be your liability if the dog commits a crime against man. Make sure you give this decision due thought and consideration. We don't want your new best friend to end his years from behind the bars of a shelter.

ARE YOU STABLE?

Of course none of us can see into the future, but you should be able to glimpse forward a couple of years. If you're getting ready to graduate school, start a job search, leave on an extended vacation, or are in some other transitional period of your life – it's obviously not the best time for you to get a dog. Wait until you don't have a lot of change in your life and you have a reasonably stable routine. Trust us, your new furry friend is going to bring enough chaos into your life that you don't need external craziness pressing on you too.

Figure 18: "Marley", taken August 2012 at Dartmoor in Devon, UK.
Photograph used with permission by Alan Dunnett.

DO YOU TRAVEL FREQUENTLY?

This question ties in with stability. Our family loves to travel. It's safe to say we travel out of town on the average of once a month, often for little weekend trips. But our choices of location and locomotion are often dictated by our family composition. We don't go to places that aren't child friendly because we like to share our lives and experiences with our daughter. Likewise, we generally choose dog friendly towns and beaches within driving distance of our home. We make those choices because we enjoy our canine family members and prefer not to kennel them or leave them with strangers longer than necessary. Plus, playing fetch in the ocean with a Patterdale Terrier always brings a smile to everyone's face – especially his!

Do you have time in your life?

What's the point of getting a dog, particularly an energetic one like a Patterdale, if no one is home for twelve hours a day? Long periods by himself will undoubtedly cause your Pat to develop behavioral issues. How could any person or animal become well-adjusted by staring at a wall, trying to hold his bladder for hours on end? Bringing up a dog correctly requires an enormous time commitment. There is no such thing as spending too much time with either your child or your dog.

Do you have the right environment?

From an ideal perspective, it would be good to have a large securely fenced in area outdoors. Living in a condominium or apartment doesn't preclude Patterdale ownership, but in such arrangements realize your furry friend will need frequent walks. These will need to happen every day, even those when you're sick with the flu and Mother Nature has decided to let the wind and rain loose upon the earth. Also keep in mind that some Patterdales can be quite vocal which may not entertain your neighbors, especially those that share interior walls. Speaking of the indoors, there needs to be room to have a crate set up, preferably in an area that can be quarantined off when necessary - where there isn't much to destroy.

Is it a good fit for your family?

Does everyone in your family want a dog? Are they committed to helping with guidance, nurturing and care requirements? If there are children in your family, are they at an age where they can respect animals? Do you have any other animals in your house? Patterdales are instinctive hunters: hamsters, rabbits, and cats beware. Do you have any other dogs now? Adding a new dog to a house with a canine or more has additional challenges. We'll talk more about them later.

Are you financially prepared?

Dogs don't have quite the fiscal requirements of human children but you still need to be prepared to pay for a good quality diet, vaccinations, and flea medication.

ARE YOU READY FOR THE LONG-TERM COMMITMENT?

The first thing to keep in mind when thinking of bringing a new dog into your family pack is that it is a long-term commitment. A Patterdale Terrier can easily have 15 years in him. Sometimes we don't know where we're going to be in 5 years much less 15. Make sure you're at a place in your life where you can be comfortable making that kind of promise to a dog.

DO YOU REALLY LOVE DOGS?

This is the most important question. You really need to love dogs when they chew up your chair leg or destroy your favorite shoes. If you love dogs you will understand the responsibility of living with one. There is time you need to make in your day for training, grooming, feeding and exercising. All of these things will try your patience and make demands on you at inopportune moments. Do you have the love to overcome?

So you took the quiz, and answered it honestly. It turns out you love dogs. You are stable. You have time. You have the space. You've thought about it long and hard. You've educated yourself on different dog breeds. You know the qualities of Patterdales and the people they would naturally complement. You've read this book and made your mind up - you're bringing a Patterdale Terrier into your life. Congratulations! You couldn't have chosen a better friend.

Now that you're getting a dog, and the best type of dog of all we might add (O.K. we're a little biased), how do you pick out the right Pat for you? First let's look at age. Should your new furry friend be a puppy or an older dog? How do you make that decision? Well let's look at your situation.

DO YOU REALLY WANT THE RESPONSIBILITY OF MOLDING A NEW LIFE?

It's a heavy question I know. All puppies are born perfect. It is then the responsibility of their human parents to support their growth and maturity into wonderful adult dogs. Human parents who do not ensure their dog's success are failures. These puppies will grow up with unacceptable behaviors and often end up unwanted and quarantined in a dog shelter.

ARE YOU WILLING TO EDUCATE YOURSELF ON BEING A GOOD PUPPY PARENT?

Dog pounds are bursting with animals whose only crime was to be chosen by untrained owners. It is your responsibility to learn how to be a responsible canine parent. It is only through appropriate conditioning of a puppy that he will grow to be an accepted member of society and a joyful addition to your life. The good news is you probably pass the test on this one. Isn't that why you're reading this book? You want to learn how to have a great relationship with your pet. You have a hunger for knowledge and a love of Patterdales.

HOW MUCH TIME WILL YOU BE ABLE TO SPEND WITH YOUR NEW DOG?

We believe one of the biggest factors in our decision to get a new dog would be the answer to this question. That first year is critical to a puppy's development. If we knew that no one would be home to help guide him for nine hours every day we would get an older dog. Puppies need a lot of our time, particularly during that first year. They are canine babies that need a great deal of direction and attention. If you honestly don't have a lot of available time we urge you to look towards getting an older dog that has already been taught manners and behavior.

ARE YOU A PATIENT PERSON?

Everyone is different. Some people are just naturally more high-strung than others. Puppies are perfect but they don't know right from wrong. Some person has to teach them that: a patient person willing to create an environment that encourages puppies to learn and grow, a patient person who realizes that puppies are impressionable and understands that each puppy is different.

If you feel comfortable with your answers to the above questions, starting off your relationship with a puppy has strong advantages. The principle benefit of which is the ability to nurture and shape your furry friend's personality, temperament, and behavior to best match life in your household. Of course molding this new little life is no easy job. Ask any mom! It requires a hefty time commitment. It requires patience and self-discipline. It requires the intelligence of how to be a good canine parent.

Figure 19: "Oscar", taken March 2014
at Victoria Park, Waterloo, Liverpool, UK.
Photograph used with permission by Richie Hooton.

Puppies need almost constant guidance for the first year, which translates into a lot of time learning how to communicate with your puppy and a lot of time educating him on your role as canine parent. We don't want this puppy growing up with behavioral issues. Also keep in mind your environment. We will teach you how to house and chew train your new best friend but we have to expect there will be mistakes made. You don't want to live in a museum or be too attached to your things especially with a Patterdale Terrier. Besides the extra time puppies will require of you they will also require you to have the knowledge of how to bring up an animal so that they will become enjoyable adults. If you decide to get a puppy your next task will be finding the right one. We'll go over that and many more puppy topics in a following chapter.

Adopting an older dog can be a wonderful choice too. If you work in an office during the day and no one will be home to train a puppy, an older dog is probably a better choice. An older dog is used to some time alone. Also, if you rescue an animal you get the wonderful feeling of giving an unwanted dog a second chance. Dogs that are over two years old already have a well-established personality, temperament and manners.

Before we leave this chapter we should spend some time talking about having more than one dog in your home. There are a lot of strong reasons for having a single dog in your family. Only-dog children get all the attention from their human pack. This usually means he will bond more closely to the members of your family. It is also much easier to take a single dog with you on park visits and vacations. Training one dog is more manageable than two or more. It is also much easier to identify an offending party. There is never a question as to who chewed up your slipper or urinated by the back door if you are a one dog home.

That being said, there are some wonderful benefits to having two dogs. They have time during the day to actually be a "dog" and do "dog" things with a like-minded friend. Please do make sure if you decide to have a second dog that he will get along with your current resident. Give them the opportunity to meet on neutral ground before you bring the new dog home. Let them get to know each other. Make sure they like each other. After that meeting you can then try the new dog at your home. You need to feel confident the two canines will get along before agreeing to an adoption. When looking for a playmate for your dog we recommend choosing a different sex partner when possible. Two same sex Patterdale Terriers can get into formidable fights when challenging rank in the household. Often these fights won't surface until your dogs are one to three years old. Households with three or more dogs we don't recommend (although we currently fall into that category). Your family may become exposed to some real dog pack dynamics and frequent bickering.

Figure 20: "Ozzy and Marley" (7 months old here), are brothers whom
uncharacteristically live together in harmony in the same home.
Photo taken in October 2012 on the Great Orme, North Wales, UK.
Photograph used with permission by Alan Dunnett.

"A dog is the only thing on earth that loves you more than he loves himself."

Josh Billings

Figure 21: "Moose", taken August 2013
at Whiteadder Reservoir, East Lothian, Scotland, UK.
Photograph used with permission by Joanne Richardson.

[5]

Adult Adoption

PRIOR TO HAVING MET my dog-loving hubby, I was not much of a dog person. Don't get me wrong - I liked dogs; I just didn't get what the big deal was all about. Watching the big dog shows such as the Westminster on television I would think to myself "these people are nuts!" before I changed the channel to a program I could better relate to like Seinfeld (a show centered on the self-absorbed). I was young and self-immersed and couldn't imagine devoting any part of myself to a dog. I used to think that dog lovers were separated from the world – lonely types that had withdrawn from human society and instead chosen to socialize with canines. I would never be one of those people.

As the old adage says: "Never say never". I look at myself back then and laugh at the dog adoring person I have become. Not only do I now have four dogs that I spend the majority of my time with, I am also a board member of our local terrier club, and an active Patterdale Terrier promoter. Yes, I am one of those crazy dog people now and I get it. I knew it was official when I agreed with the statement – "The more people I meet, the more I like dogs". If the old Jennifer could only see me now...

GIVING LIFE A SECOND CHANCE

So you've been honest with yourself and realistically because of your commitments, to work or other priorities, you cannot promise the large amount of time needed for the development of a new puppy. You have decided to adopt an older dog, wonderful! Now on to the next question, how do you pick out your new pal? It is best to use both your mind and your heart to make this choice.

In general, the two traits we warn against in an adult dog are fear and aggression. Both of these traits are spawned from trust issues that can take a great deal of time, patience, and advanced training to overcome in a mature canine. There is an appropriate expression that goes "Trust takes years to build and only seconds to shatter". To illustrate this point to a smaller degree, we have a terrier that had her head caught by a swinging door when she was five months old. That moment began her fear of doorways. It has taken us a great deal of time and effort to help her overcome that fear; baby steps of propping a door open. All the way at first; then slowly each day making the opening smaller and smaller, until now when she will actually push the door with her nose to open it. This progression has taken us three years to reach with daily exercises. This wasn't even a serious fear issue.

Aggression is another tough one that involves building trust. We were working with a rescue group that had a female Patterdale Terrier that was extremely dog aggressive. When working on her rehabilitation it was very important to create an environment where she could not fail. Working with her and other dogs required close supervision and always a secure lead. When humans made errors and failed to pay attention, bloody battles were the result. These cases are best left to professionals.

How do you check for potential trouble traits? First, pay attention to his social etiquette. How does your new prospect react when he first meets your family? Is he friendly and enjoy being pet and handled by everyone? That's a good sign. Does he cower or shows signs of fear? Not so good. Pay attention to how he interacts with all kinds of new people: women, men, and children. It is also a good idea to see how he interrelates with other dogs; you will probably be taking him on walks to the park where he is certain to come into contact with other humans and canines. It is vital to know how he will behave in these situations. Touch the dog all over, including his face, ears, paws, belly, and tail. Practice restraining the dog and picking him up. Look for any telltale signs of fear or aggression. How does he do on a leash walk? We would be wary of dogs that are afraid of a leash and collar. Ideally he will walk comfortably at your side. But many Patterdale Terriers are strong leash pullers and that's not necessarily a reason to cross your new friend off the list.

How are his living quarters? Is there a potential housetraining problem you need to be aware of? When you first meet him is he calm and interested or a hyper, barking spaz? Keep in mind that Patterdales do tend to be more on the energetic side; we would be more concerned about a lethargic dog. Check and see if the dog knows any commands like sit, come, down, and stay. Training older dogs to walk on a leash, how to sit, and where to relieve himself are generally not exceedingly difficult. They just require someone with patience that can communicate proper manners to your new friend.

Figure 22: "Nogger", taken June 2011 in Ulm, Germany.
Photograph used with permission by Ralph Rückert.

Once you are comfortable that you've found a new adult dog to be your new best friend, what do you do when you bring him home? You are going to bring your new addition into your family and he needs to know the rules of the house and appropriate behavior. The first few weeks in your home are very important in establishing this appropriate canine conduct.

So what do we need to teach him straightaway? First we need to make sure our new friend understands that people are good and can be trusted. Second, we need to train him the appropriate place to relieve himself. Third, we need to teach him how to calm himself (our Patterdales often make this one challenging!). Finally, we need to teach him which toys are his.

To prepare for his homecoming we need to set up a safe area. This is an area where we'll he'll spend the majority of his time for the first couple days, and in the future where he'll be restricted when you're not available to watch him. Ideally this will be a room blocked off with baby gates. An exercise pen set up in your home can also be utilized for this purpose. It is preferable to have his safe area over tile or some easily cleaned floor surface – your kitchen may be a good choice. If you choose to use a room, it's best to use the walk through baby gates when possible. Metal is the ideal choice of material as it is less likely to be chewed on. His crate belongs in the safe area. Use either a wire kennel or an airline plastic-sided type. The size of the crate for an adult Patterdale is around 24" x 20" x 20" or slightly smaller. Put something comfortable in his crate for sleeping. You can use a crate pad, blanket, towels, or an old pillow. It's best to use something that is easy to wash. Finally you'll want to add a no-spill stainless steel water bowl to his safe area and a dog-safe chew bone or two. We employ natural antlers and Nylabones for Patterdale chew toys. It's a good idea to rotate toys to keep them interesting. We didn't mention a food bowl and we'll explain why later.

Now that we have his safe area prepared let's go get our new best friend. The key thing to keep in mind when bringing home our new furry friend is trust. We want to gain his and develop ours in him. To keep his trust we'll introduce people, places, and things to him gradually and associate them with positive experiences. To develop our trust in him we'll limit his opportunities to make mistakes until he learns the rules.

Your relationship begins on the car ride home so let's start this off right. Bring his crate when you go to pick him up. Check his reaction to his new bed. Throw an interesting treat inside like a piece of string cheese or hot dog. Does he just walk right in through the open door, eat it and walk out? Perfect. Is he afraid to walk in? If so, do not start the relationship with a bad experience of locking him in something he's fearful of and shoving him in the back of a moving vehicle. That could train him to be terrified of his bed. If he exhibits no fear of the crate let's put our little friend inside with maybe a familiar toy and drive him home. If he is frightened of the crate and it is a short drive home have someone strong and calm (key being calm) hold him by his collar for the ride home. We shouldn't need to point out that the driver should not be the one holding the dog! If your dog is crazy excited when you start the car and begin to move - it's best to put him in the crate, regardless. Don't risk an auto accident on the beginning of your journey together.

We know when you get a new dog the first thing you want to do is show him to all your family and friends. Instead, start by making introductions to his immediate family and teaching him his first lessons. When you get home, put him on a leash, trying to keep calm. Then take him to where he will need to relieve himself and praise him when he does. Next, play with your new pal in his safe area. One fun introduction game is to have the family stand around the room and take turns calling him. When he comes to each person, they can give him kibble from their hand and praise. Use food and praise to implant positive associations with his new family. Already, he's getting great experiences learning where to potty and that people are good. On this first day, we also need to teach him about his bed. Leave the crate door open and throw in a particularly interesting treat and get him used to walking in and out of the create without fear. As his comfort level with the crate becomes greater, slowly add in closing the door: just with your hand for a second, then latching it and increasing the time before re-opening. Remember the name of the game is to go slowly. For crate training exercises, avoid excitement by not making a big deal when he is let out of the crate. Crate time should be a calm time.

Figure 23: "Shamus", taken in 2009 in CA, USA.
Photograph used with permission by Anglo-American Patterdales.

Continued on this first day take him out frequently to eliminate and praise him when he does. Now another trick we need to teach our friend is that it's O.K. for us to leave his room without him and he should be calm until we return. To teach him this we're going to give him a job. For this we will employ a toy that can be filled with treats like a kibble dispensing ball. Fill his ball with kibble and roll it to show him how food comes out. Now put it down and let him play with it in his safe area. While he's working on it ignore him and calmly walk outside the gate and then back in. Gradually increase the time your away and make it so he can't see you. We're training him to enjoy alone periods.

It's not a good idea to let your new pal have free run of the house when you're not available. Bored Patterdales are quite capable of causing significant damage. We have a dining room table, numerous shoes, and countless stuffed animals that have met their fate in this way. Your Pat will come to know his safe area as a place to be comfortable and calm when you aren't available and will also learn that you will always return there to get him. We're teaching him those principles and giving him a job to get fed. If you choose to feed your dog with kibble we recommend feeding him exclusively from treat balls when possible. After feeding him, pick up the ball when he's done so he comes to know it's a special toy only for meals.

We need to take a moment to advise against leaving your dog outside while you are not at home (even if you have a fenced in yard). This is particularly critical during the first months while you are getting to know him. Patterdales are the most prodigious diggers in the canine world. There are very few yards that he will not be able to find his way out of given enough unsupervised time.\

To continue your doggie education, there are two excellent animal behaviorists we recommend to help you further develop your new Patterdale into a wonderful balanced canine. The first is Dr. Ian Dunbar, who at the time of this publication maintains the www.DogStarDaily.com website. Dr. Dunbar has outlined particularly strong lessons of errorless house-training and feeding only through toys that we heartily recommend in *Before & After You Get Your Puppy* (Dunbar, 2004). The second animal behaviorist needs no introduction. Cesar Millan has numerous books and videos that are all excellent resources. His work on solving challenging dog habits through calm, assertive energy is well-known and proven effective.

We hope that this chapter has helped you decide if adult adoption is the right choice for you. There are so many unwanted adult dogs that need homes today. While puppies are always hard to resist, they do require time to school and that someone be around to take care of them and train them, especially in the first year. If your life requires that you be away from your home during the day, an adult dog just might be the right choice for you. Regardless of whether you decide on a puppy or adult dog to take home, we hope that you will do your homework to create the greatest life for both you and your new best friend.

Figure 24: "Millie" and "Denzil", taken February 2014 at Poole in Dorset, UK.
Photograph used with permission by Gareth Dancey.

"There is no psychiatrist in the world like a puppy licking your face."

Bern Williams

Figure 25: "Hera" and "Samson", taken February 2012 in Ruskin, FL, USA.
Photograph used with permission by Anglo-American Patterdales.

[6]

Puppy Talk

GROWING UP, I never had a dog. Well, when I was in grade school we entertained our neighbor's Dachshund. He was always on the loose, free and frisky, running into our house when he needed to seek shelter from a storm. This arrangement seemed to work for both the dog and us.

When I was in high school my mother brought home a Himalayan Ragdoll cat. The cat never seemed to enjoy my company, as much as I tried to befriend the longhaired snob. Even still, when I graduated college and moved out on my own, I believed a cat would be the pet for me. Needing little maintenance, they seemed matched for my busy lifestyle. I adopted an abandoned cat from a local rescue. I fed and pet him while I watched TV after work. We had a peaceful cohabitation arrangement.

I moved on, married, and found a house in the suburbs. Like many couples who move to the 'burbs, we went looking for our first child, a puppy. We found him at a shelter, a small shorthaired terrier, completely out of place below the jumping baby huskies. There he was, a little button-eared four month-old puppy, fighting hard to get noticed. I couldn't take my eyes off him. I reached my arms inside the pen and he jumped into them. If you've ever had that special feeling about a dog, then you will know what I am going to say. He was the one. He needed to be rescued; and as it turned out, so did I.

Captain never ran out of gas. He was a tireless ball fetcher. Your arm would tire long before he would ever stop retrieving. And the minute you stopped throwing, you would come to regret that decision. You would either have a crazed dog digging a goliath hole on the beach, or you would have a frantic dog poised and panting, awaiting your next launch into the backyard. He was a digger, a jumper, and an all-around hyperactive spaz. Looking back at my life, he was one of my best friends.

Little did I know at the time that the decision to pick up that little terrier puppy and bring him home would be a life-changing experience. He had so much energy, and was an inspiration in making the most of his life in such a short time. Never tiring, never inattentive, he was always there for me. And in some crazy way, I think he still is.

PUPPY LOVE

We spoke in a previous chapter about choices. Maybe you have made the choice to bring a new Patterdale Terrier puppy into your home. A puppy is an absolutely wonderful choice if you have the time and commitment to bring him up correctly. We would be remiss if we did not stress one last time the magnitude of this decision. Puppies grow rapidly in that first year and there are several behavioral attitudes that need to be taught during that time or they will be very difficult to correct in his later life. Puppies that grow up with behavioral problems often times end up unwanted and abandoned. We know that you have the best of intentions and by reading this book you are getting the education you need to be an excellent puppy parent!

Figure 26: "Uno", taken in January, 2013 in Ruskin, FL, USA.
Photograph used with permission by Anglo-American Patterdales.

There are three topics we need to cover to prepare for puppy raising. They are home preparation, puppy selection, and important early behavior training. Hopefully, you'll read this entire chapter, or better the entire book, before you bring home your new furry baby.

Home Preparation

So let's start with prepping your home. The arrangements for bringing home a canine puppy are not that different from bringing home a human baby:

- A safe room is established to be his
- A doctor is selected
- A bed, special food and toys are purchased
- Educational activities and feeding schedules are planned
- The home is "puppy proofed" where dangerous and fragile items are removed from reach

Obtaining the proper supplies and puppy proofing your home is essential for both the safety of the puppy and the sanity of the people that live there. Taking the time to puppy proof your house and yard is a simple way to create a safe, friendly environment for the newest member of your pack.

You'll want to do some shopping before you bring your puppy home since most of the supplies you will purchase can be used right from the start. At the very least your new friend will need a crate, water bowl, chew toys, a collar and a leash. Whenever possible select durable items as Patterdale puppies have boundless energy and an aptitude for destruction.

Let's start with his sleeping quarters. For that we'll need a crate. Think of this as your puppy's crib. Your puppy will grow up knowing his crate as his safe den. We will help him always feel safe and secure in his den. You will use his crate as his sleeping quarters, to potty train, and to keep him comfortable while travelling (wouldn't it be nice if we could travel with our own bed?). So how do you choose an appropriate crate? The first guidance we will offer is to avoid soft-sided crates. Patterdale Terriers are aggressive chewers and these crates aren't secure. We also advise against wood crates, as they're heavy and easily damaged by chewing. The other two major varieties are the plastic airline type and wire crates. The choice between these two is largely personal preference. While the plastic crates can be used for airline travel, the wire crates offer more ventilation and often come with a divider which makes potty training easier. In our house, we have chosen to utilize heavy-duty wire crates (Midwest Ultima Pro model number 724UP). When picking out your crate make sure it is the appropriate size for your puppy when he becomes an adult, look for something around 24" x 20" x 20" or a little smaller for your Patterdale as a general guideline. Now this crate will be too large for your puppy at first so we need to make the interior dimensions smaller until he grows into it. As we mentioned, one of the benefits of the all-metal crates is that they often come with dividers for this very purpose. If you don't have a divider you'll have to make his den smaller using an appropriate solid object to fill the space, like a milk crate. Make the interior of his den just large enough him to lie down, stand up and turn around.

As for bedding, keep in mind that whatever you use may end up in shreds. You may want to wait until your puppy is out of his chewing phase before purchasing anything nice. Old blankets or towels work well and can be washed and easily changed out while your furry friend is potty training.

While he's a puppy you'll want to have a quarantined safe area where you can keep him when you can't keep your eye on him (mischievous puppies given free reign of the house will cause damage). You can use an exercise pen for this purpose. We have our kitchen restricted with baby gates to serve our safe area need. On a side note, the baby gates with built in doors are wonderful for high-traffic areas. Continually stepping over gates quickly becomes tiresome and dangerous. If you do decide to go with the baby gate approach we would advise against wooden ones. They may look nice at first but it doesn't take long for a puppy to chew on them. It is appropriate to have his safe area over tile or some easily cleaned floor surface and keep anything you don't want him to chew, out of this area. Set up his crate in this safe area.

You'll need a quality water bowl for your new furry friend. The best material for water bowls is stainless steel. Stainless steel bowls cannot be chewed up or ingested. They are easy to clean and disinfect, and they won't absorb smells. Ceramic and glass bowls can break into small, sharp pieces so they are not ideal for new and rowdy puppies. Try and purchase the no-tip bowls to prevent against spills. I'm sure you noticed we didn't mention a food bowl. There are reasons for this that we'll go into when we talk about feeding. When you bring home your new best friend you'll keep his water bowl in his safe area too.

Figure 27: Stainless steel bowls are best for dogs, particularly puppies.

You will also need suitable chew toys to keep his chewing energy focused appropriately. The key word here is durable. We recommend Nylabones (particularly the Galileo line), tough rubber Kongs (we love the Kong Stuff-a-Ball), and deer antlers. Make sure that no matter what you choose, it is safe and fun. We also like the Kong Wubba's and ordinary racquetballs for indoor amusement. You'll need to keep your puppy interested in his toys. Show him that his toys are the best and most exciting things to chew on. This will save your sofa, your shoes, and your hands. It's a good idea to frequently switch out toys so your little friend doesn't get bored with them.

You will want to select a light, thin, nylon collar and leash. You will want to put a collar on your puppy within the first day or so home. Make sure it is not too loose around his neck as a little leg can get caught in the collar very easily (especially since it is a new and he may try to take it off). Secure the collar so you can just fit a couple of fingers under it. Also, no puppy or dog should be without an ID tag on his collar. In addition to this identification, you may also decide to implant a microchip in your puppy.

Dog microchips are the size of grain of rice. They are implanted by way of a syringe between the dog's shoulder blades. This is very similar to a vaccination and after implantation the dog should feel no pain or discomfort. The microchip can be detected with a handheld wand, which displays a unique alphanumeric code that is registered for your dog. This is a one-time implant as there are no batteries or such in the microchip that would need to be replaced.

Of course your new furry friend will need food. Select a high quality small kibble food. We are going to go into diets in a later part of this book, but we recommend starting your new pup on kibble. Most likely that's what your breeder used during weaning. You don't want to upset his stomach with new food as he joins his new household. If possible, get a bag of the kibble your breeder was feeding him. If you prefer to switch to a different food, make sure you gradually wean the puppy onto the new formula by adding increasing amounts of the new brand to his current kibble over time. This can prevent or reduce stomach and intestinal upset. Once your new friend reaches six months of age you may choose to follow one of the diets outlined in the diet chapter.

A few other items you may want to keep on hand are a nail clipper, a natural bristle brush, and a chemical cleaner/deodorizer for accidents. It's not necessary to spend a lot of money on puppy products. Once you have the essentials, wait until your buddy comes home to see what else he needs. You don't want to buy a bunch of stuff that will never be used.

Once your supplies are in order, you will need to make sure that you puppy proof both your home and your yard. Every area that your puppy might be exposed to should be considered. Get close to the ground and look around, checking for things that might be inviting to chew. Check every nook and cranny for dangerous items. This includes under and behind furniture and tables or any other dark place a puppy may choose to go. Patterdales are fearless, particularly in regards to exploring dark, tight spaces. We sequestered off our kitchen for a safe area and came in one afternoon with no sight of our little Patterdale son. At first we thought he had somehow managed to jump the baby gate. After a thorough search we found that he was still in the kitchen. He had simply wedged himself between the fridge and cabinet and was sniffing something there - just happy as can be. What he was sniffing under the fridge we probably didn't want to know!

We'll begin by puppy proofing the house. Move houseplants so that they are out of your puppies reach. Patterdales are aggressive diggers; I can't tell you how often we would catch one our dogs digging in a houseplant. We started putting large river stones over the soil in our big planters to discourage their interest. You also need to watch where you keep your shoes and dirty laundry. While it might seem like a good idea to let your puppy chew on an old shoe, you will not think it is funny when he finds a new one to chew on. He won't know the difference between the two so it's best to establish good habits from the beginning.

Secure tablecloths or other hanging items. Move items from coffee tables and other low furniture. Puppies have a tendency to put their paws on things. Make sure there is nothing dangerous on the floor that he can knock over. Make certain that you secure anything breakable. It could be harmful to your puppy and stressful for you, particularly if the item is expensive.

Close cupboards and make sure that hazardous materials such as cleaning products, medications, painting supplies, and other poisons are not within his reach. Make certain that there are no phone wires or electric cords he can chew on. If you cannot move the wires, you can wrap them in plastic sheathing or PVC tubing.

Teach your children to put away their toys and stuffed animals. A puppy is not able to distinguish between a child's toy and his own. This can lead to the crying of small children when their favorite plaything is destroyed. Our daughter is an insatiable stuffed animal hoarder, on close inspection you can see many of her little plush pals are missing eyes and noses because she doesn't always put them out of reach.

Your Patterdale puppy knows instinctively that wood is good to chew. Protect anything made of wood including table and chair legs. If possible, do not leave them alone with wood chairs or tables. In our kitchen where we keep the dogs when we're busy (the safe area) we have an iron table and chair set. Of course, that didn't stop our Pat Voodoo from chewing on the corner of a cabinet when he was a puppy. If possible, try to make the area that he will remain in when you are not able to watch him one that has items that are safe for him to gnaw on.

After you have made your house a safe place for your puppy it is time to move on to the yard. Put away garden hoses and yard tools. Make sure that your children have not left any small plastic toys lying around. Look for anything your puppy can fall into or put in his mouth.

Figure 28: Be sure to make your yard a safe place for your new pup to play.
"Milo", taken in the Spring of 2013 in
the Silverstone woods, Northamptonshire, UK.
Photograph used with permission by Tex Marshall.

Even if you are planning on teaching your Patterdale to swim, you need to block access to the pool, if you have one. Dogs can drown in a pool if they don't know where the steps are to get out. Block other hazardous spaces by fencing off any areas you don't want your puppy to be in and make sure he can't squeeze through the fence. Put away chemicals and yard poisons such as lawn fertilizers and insecticides.

Patterdales are voracious diggers. Check your fencing for escape routes and make sure there's nowhere for your puppy to crawl under. Check for gaps around gates and fence sections and make sure your puppy can't get his head stuck. It's a good idea when possible to bury part of the fencing to keep your friend from digging out. You want to train your puppy early that he can't escape from your yard. As soon as he finds a way to escape once, he won't soon forget it. He'll go back to the place he escaped from repeatedly and also start looking in earnest for other routes to freedom. When a Patterdale sets his mind that he can do something, he will. It's one of the amazing yet frustrating characteristics of the Patterdale type.

Puppy Selection

Now that you have prepared your home, for your new little bundle of joy, you need to turn your attention to puppy selection, as this is one of those important choices we talked about. So how do you choose a great puppy? The first step to choosing a great puppy is identifying a great breeder. Quality breeders will produce quality pups. A superior breeder is constantly striving to improve the Patterdale type. They care about the animals they produce and where they are placed. They keep up with news of pups they produce long after they leave their home (our breeder keeps in regular contact with us via Facebook and regional terrier trials we both attend).

A responsible breeder does not over-breed. They propagate for a purpose and only when they are certain they have appropriate homes screened for their puppies. They only breed dogs that are at least two years old, when the quality of the parents is proven. Good breeders are not interested in financial gain from breeding animals. They provide the female and her puppies a healthy, calm environment. They make certain each puppy is socialized and stimulated. When the puppy goes to its new home they remain available to the new owners to answer questions and offer advice. A quality breeder will take a dog back if for some reason you can no longer keep it.

A responsible breeder will interview you as a potential Patterdale owner. They'll want to know about your home environment and your understanding of the Patterdale type. They'll want to make sure you're educated about Patterdale Terriers.

You want a puppy that was raised inside a home. A pup raised inside has already become accustomed to the noises and schedules that come with living with a family. He will be more easily integrated into your home. He's heard and seen televisions and vacuum cleaners. A pup raised in kennels isn't being brought up by a breeder looking to socialize his animals. It is wise to avoid these breeders.

Figure 29: "Wilbur" and "Charlotte", taken in 2009 in Ruskin, FL, USA.
Photograph used with permission by Anglo-American Patterdales.

So how do we find a quality breeder? First, you'll want to reach out to the Patterdale organization that serves your area. Contact them and compile a list of suggested breeders. Then set up phone interviews with the different breeders. Ask questions - a good breeder loves talking about Patterdales and their own in particular. Ask why they breed dogs? Why they breed Patterdale Terriers specifically? Do they have any breedings coming up that you could potentially be on the list for? Why are they breeding that litter? What is the ancestry of the litter? Has that pair been mated in the past? Is there access to both parents for a visit? You shouldn't be put off if they only have the female on site, as it is not unusual to employ stud services. Ask if the puppies are kept in the home. Ask what training they do with their puppies. Are they exposed to children? Ask for healthcare advice: vaccines, worming, fleas, diet, and raising guidance. Ask for their contract. A good breeder should have a contract that defines the breeder policies regarding health guarantees, return rules, etc. Do they have references of puppy placements that you can follow up with? And do follow up. Call the other owners and find out their experience with their dog and that breeder.

Once you start to feel comfortable with a breeder or two make an appointment to see their facilities. Their home and dog runs should be clean and well maintained.

You should be able to handle their older dogs on premises and make sure they are healthy, well groomed, social and behaved. Be wary if any dogs are fearful of strangers, all dogs on the premises should be people friendly. Understand that a good breeder may not allow you to handle new puppies, as they may be concerned of introducing illness to the newborns. But you should still be able to assess that puppies are social and trained.

So now you have identified a quality breeder. You have established a relationship with this person and the two of you have planned for your new pup to come from a particular upcoming mating. Great! This is exciting.

So now there is the next decision to be made. Do you want a boy or girl? This is really personal preference. Personality of puppies has little to do with their gender. The only thing we will stress is that if this is to be a second dog for your home, it is probably best to choose an opposite sex companion.

Your breeder should know what you are looking for in a dog: whether hunter, ball catcher, racer, or showman. She may select which pup you should take home. She may decide to let you have a choice from some of the puppies in the litter. Here we go, another big decision. How do you know which one to choose? The bright side of this decision is that if you have done your breeder homework, they will most likely all be wonderful choices. But let's make a thoughtful selection.

You may not think much about it but there are many different characteristics of a dog's personality, much like our own. The ones you want to see maximized in your new furry friend will depend on you and your expectations. So if you are given the option of choosing your puppy, try to pick the best one from the litter for you.

Figure 30: "Oscar", taken April 2014 at Formby Point, Merseyside, UK.
Photograph used with permission by Richie Hooton.

PUPPY APTITUDE TEST

Jack and Wendy Volhard wrote the quintessential puppy aptitude test and have made it available on their website www.volhard.com and in their book *Dog Training for Dummies* (Volhard, 2010). We highly recommend following their guidelines if you will be choosing your next puppy from a litter. The Volhard's tests examine ten different characteristics, which are of interest to puppy parents. The information is reproduced here with their permission. The tendencies tested are as follows:

1. SOCIAL ATTRACTION. Degree of social attraction to people, confidence or dependence.
2. FOLLOWING. Willingness to follow a person.
3. RESTRAINT. Degree of dominant or submissive tendency, and ease of handling in difficult situations.
4. SOCIAL DOMINANCE. Degree of acceptance of social dominance by a person.
5. ELEVATION. Degree of accepting dominance while in a position of no control, such as at the veterinarian or groomer.
6. RETRIEVING. Degree of willingness to do something for you. Together with Social Attraction and Following a key indicator for ease or difficulty in training.
7. TOUCH SENSITIVITY. Degree of sensitivity to touch and a key indicator to the type of training equipment required.
8. SOUND SENSITIVITY. Degree of sensitivity to sound, such as loud noises or thunderstorms.
9. SIGHT SENSITIVITY. Degree of response to a moving object, such as chasing bicycles, children or squirrels.
10. STABILITY. Degree of startle response to a strange object.

Here are the testing ground rules:
- Puppies should be tested as close to 49th day from birth (age 7 weeks) as possible.
- The testing is done in a location unfamiliar to the puppies. This does not mean they have to taken away from home. A 10-foot square area is perfectly adequate, such as a room in the house where the puppies have not been.
- The puppies are tested one at a time.
- There are no other dogs or people, except the scorer and the tester, in the testing area.
- The puppies do not know the tester.
- The scorer is a disinterested third party and not the person interested in selling you a puppy.
- The scorer is unobtrusive and positions him or herself so he or she can observe the puppies' responses without having to move.
- The puppies are tested before they are fed.
- The puppies are tested when they are at their liveliest.

- Do not try to test a puppy that is not feeling well.
- Puppies should not be tested the day of or the day after being vaccinated.
- Only the first response counts.
- Tests are performed consecutively and in the order given.
- Each test is scored separately and interpreted on its own.
- During testing maintain a positive, upbeat and friendly attitude toward the puppies. Try to get each puppy to interact with you to bring out the best in him or her. Make the test a pleasant experience for the puppy.

Here are the tests:

1. SOCIAL ATTRACTION. The owner or caretaker of the puppies places it in the test area about four feet from the tester and then leaves the test area. The tester kneels down and coaxes the puppy to come to him or her by encouragingly and gently clapping hands and calling. The tester must coax the puppy in the opposite direction from where it entered the test area. [Hint: Lean backward, sitting on your heels instead of leaning forward toward the puppy. Keep your hands close to your body encouraging the puppy to come to you instead of trying to reach for the puppy.]

2. FOLLOWING. The tester stands up and slowly walks away encouraging the puppy to follow. [Hint: Make sure the puppy sees you walk away and get the puppy to focus on you by lightly clapping your hands and using verbal encouragement to get the puppy to follow you. Do not lean over the puppy.]

3. RESTRAINT. The tester crouches down and gently rolls the puppy on its back and holds it on its back for 30 seconds. [Hint: Hold the puppy down without applying too much pressure. The object is not to keep it on its back but to test its response to being placed in that position.]

4. SOCIAL DOMINANCE. Let the puppy stand up or sit and gently stroke it from the head to the back while you crouch beside it. See if it will lick your face, an indication of a forgiving nature. Continue stroking until you see a behavior you can score. [Hint: When you crouch next to the puppy avoid leaning or hovering over the puppy. Have the puppy at your side with both of you facing in the same direction.]

5. ELEVATION DOMINANCE. The tester cradles the puppy with both hands, supporting the puppy under its chest and gently lifts its front two feet off the ground and holds it there for 30 seconds.

6. RETRIEVING. The tester crouches beside the puppy and attracts its attention with a crumpled up piece of paper. When the puppy shows some interest, the tester throws the paper no more than four feet in front of the puppy encouraging it to retrieve the paper.

7. TOUCH SENSITIVITY. The tester locates the webbing of one the puppy's front paws and presses it lightly between his index finger and thumb. The tester gradually increases pressure while counting to ten and stops when the puppy pulls away or shows signs of discomfort.

8. SOUND SENSITIVITY. The puppy is placed in the center of the testing area and an assistant stationed at the perimeter makes a sharp noise, such as banging a metal spoon on the bottom of a metal pan.

9. SIGHT SENSITIVITY. The puppy is placed in the center of the testing area. The tester ties a string around a bath towel and jerks it across the floor, two feet away from the puppy.

10. STABILITY. An umbrella is opened about five feet from the puppy and gently placed on the ground.

Scoring the Results:

Following are the responses and score assigned to each particular response. The tester will need to make a judgment call on some of a puppy's responses.

SOCIAL ATTRACTION

Came readily, tail up, jumped, bit at hands	1
Came readily, tail up, pawed, licked at hands	2
Came readily, tail up	3
Came readily, tail down	4
Came hesitantly, tail down	5
Didn't come at all	6

FOLLOWING

Followed readily, tail up, got underfoot, bit at feet	1
Followed readily, tail up, got underfoot	2
Followed readily, tail up	3
Followed readily, tail down	4
Followed hesitantly, tail down	5
Did not follow or went away	6

RESTRAINT

Struggled fiercely, flailed, bit — 1
Struggled fiercely, flailed — 2
Settled, struggled, settled with some eye contact — 3
Struggled, then settled — 4
No struggle — 5
No struggle, strained to avoid eye contact — 6

SOCIAL DOMINANCE

Jumped, pawed, bit, growled — 1
Jumped, pawed — 2
Cuddled up to tester and tried to lick face — 3
Squirmed, licked at hands — 4
Rolled over, licked at hands — 5
Went away and stayed away — 6

ELEVATION DOMINANCE

Struggled fiercely, tried to bite — 1
Struggled fiercely — 2
Struggled, settled, struggled, settled — 3
No struggle, relaxed — 4
No struggle, body stiff — 5
No struggle, froze — 6

RETRIEVING

Chased object, picked it up and ran away — 1
Chased object, stood over it and did not return — 2
Chased object, picked it up and returned with it to tester — 3
Chased object and returned without it to tester — 4
Started to chase object, lost interest — 5
Does not chase object — 6

TOUCH SENSITIVITY

8-10 count before response — 1
6-8 count before response — 2
5-6 count before response — 3
3-5 count before response — 4
2-3 count before response — 5
1-2 count before response — 6

SOUND SENSITIVITY

Listened, located sound and ran toward it barking — 1

Listened, located sound and walked slowly toward it	2
Listened, located sound and showed curiosity	3
Listened and located sound	4
Cringed, backed off and hid behind tester	5
Ignored sound and showed no curiosity	6

SIGHT SENSITIVITY

Looked, attacked and bit object	1
Looked and put feet on object and put mouth on it	2
Looked with curiosity and attempted to investigate, tail up	3
Looked with curiosity, tail down	4
Ran away or hid behind tester	5
Hid behind tester	6

STABILITY

Looked and ran to the umbrella, mouthing or biting it	1
Looked and walked to the umbrella, smelling it cautiously	2
Looked and went to investigate	3
Sat and looked, but did not move toward the umbrella	4
Showed little or no interest	5
Ran away from the umbrella	6

This is how to interpret the scores:

- Mostly 1's. This pup is not shy about his intentions and has pack leader written all over him. Has a predisposition to be aggressive to people and other dogs and will bite. Should only be placed into a very experienced home where the dog will be trained and worked on a regular basis. [Top Dog Tips: Stay away from the puppy with a lot of 1's or 2's. It has lots of leadership aspirations and may be difficult to manage. This puppy needs an experienced home. Not good with children.]

- Mostly 2's. Leadership aspirations. May be hard to manage and has the capacity to bite. Has lots of self-confidence. Should not be placed in an inexperienced home. Too unruly to be good with children and elderly people, or other animals. Needs strict schedule, loads of exercise and lots of training. Has the potential to be a great show dog with someone who understands dog behavior.

- Mostly 3's. Can be a high-energy dog and may need lots of exercise. Good with people and other animals. Can be a bit of a handful to live with. Needs training, does very well at it and learns quickly. Great dog for second time owner.

- Mostly 4's. The kind of dog that makes the perfect pet. Best choice for the first time owner. Rarely will buck for a promotion in the family. Easy to train, and rather quiet. Good with elderly people, children, although may need protection from the children. Choose this pup, take it to obedience classes, and you'll be the star, without having to do too much work! [Top Dog Tips: The puppy with mostly 3's and 4's can be quite a handful, but should be good with children and does well with training. Energy needs to be dispersed with plenty of exercise.]

- Mostly 5's. Fearful, shy and needs special handling. Will run away at the slightest stress in its life. Strange people, strange places, different floor or ground surfaces may upset it. Often afraid of loud noises and terrified of thunder storms. When you greet it upon your return, may submissively urinate. Needs a very special home where the environment doesn't change too much and where there are no children. Best for a quiet, elderly couple. If cornered and cannot get away, has a tendency to bite. [Top Dog Tips: Avoid the puppy with several 6's. It is so independent it doesn't need you or anyone. He is his own person and unlikely to bond to you.]

- Mostly 6's. So independent that he doesn't need you or other people. Doesn't care if he is trained or not - he is his own person. Unlikely to bond to you, since he doesn't need you. A great guard dog for gas stations! Do not take this puppy and think you can change him into a lovable bundle - you can't, so leave well enough alone.

Few puppies will test with all 2's or all 3's - there will be a mixture of scores. For that first time, wonderfully easy to train, potential star, look for a puppy that scores with mostly 4's and 3's. Don't worry about the score on Touch Sensitivity - you can compensate for that with the right training equipment. [Tidbits: It's hard not to become emotional when picking a puppy - they are all so cute, soft and cuddly. Remind yourself that this dog is going to be with you for 8 to 16 years. Don't hesitate to step back a little to contemplate your decision. Sleep on it and review it in the light of day.]

Avoid the puppy with a score of 1 on the Restraint and Elevation tests. This puppy will be too much for the first time owner. It's a lot more fun to have a good dog: one that is easy to train, one you can live with and one you can be proud of, than one that is a constant struggle.

Figure 31: "Sahara", taken September 2014 in Atlanta, GA, USA.

IMPORTANT EARLY BEHAVIOR TRAINING

So now you have picked him out, your perfect Patterdale puppy. You've also puppy-proofed your home and stocked needed supplies. Now it's time for your new best friend's homecoming! Remember your pup has probably never left his home, mother, and siblings for the first eight weeks of his life. We are assuming you're bringing your pup home at 8 weeks of age. Time before that should be spent with his littermates and mother.

Homecoming should be as comfortable and stress-free as possible. Make calm introductions to his new family including any household pets. Keep visitors from stopping by while he gets comfortable in his new home. The goal during these early introductions to the sights and sounds of his new forever home is to be a positive experience. We want our new furry friend to be around all the normal hustle and bustle of our lives without developing fear and bad behavior problems. These early days are critical for his development and he is relying on you to rear him appropriately.

Try and make it easy for him to do the right thing and difficult to make mistakes. Mistakes will happen and when they do you can use them as an opportunity for learning. Accomplish these goals by understanding your puppy's needs, anticipating his actions and leading him to the correct result.

Being a smaller breed, Patterdale puppies have very small stomachs and it is difficult for them to get adequate nutrition without regular meals. Allow your puppy to eat his dry puppy food for about five to ten minutes and then withdraw any remaining food. If you have more than one puppy, give them separate spaces for mealtime so they don't feel the need to compete for food. As for a meal schedule, feed him at least four meals per day until twelve weeks of age, and then feed at least three times per day until his first birthday.

Free feeding is not recommended. Feeding regular meals of his dry puppy food allows the gastric juices to rest and helps your puppy to be eager for the next meal. Small breeds tend toward obesity in adult hood, so limiting intake is a good rule to establish early. Good nutrition may be the most important factor affecting any dog's health, but especially growing puppies. So, take time to do the research and feed the best dry puppy food you can.

Plan to start training your puppy on arrival. This is the perfect time to start building habits for house training and obedience training. The first few days will offer lots of opportunities to praise good behavior and establish you as leader. One of the most important things to remember is to not punish your puppy. It's too soon to discipline for any behavior. Think of your puppy like a newborn baby. He has no idea what you expect of him and punishing him will only confuse him. We need to focus on positive reinforcement.

As soon as you bring your puppy home, take him to the area you've established for bathroom breaks. Taking him out to the same place each time will get him used to that area and he will eventually know what to do when he gets there. Wait until he uses the bathroom then praise him to start the housetraining process on a good note.

When you bring your puppy inside, let him explore in a safe area on his own for a while. If you've taken the time to puppy proof your home, he should be safe but keep your eye on him. If your puppy finds something unsafe or chews on an object that's not his, don't punish him. Try to exchange the object for something you've designated as a chew toy.

You will want to start using the puppies name right away and abundantly. Whenever your puppy focuses his attention on you, either by looking up at you or following you, say his name cheerfully. This connects his name to paying attention to you and marks you as leader. This will come in very handy when you begin obedience training.

Your puppy will need several naps each day. You should establish different areas in your home for different puppy activities including nap times. Create a closed off area somewhere close by to keep an eye on him, such as the kitchen. Put his crate in this area with some comfortable bedding. Don't force him into his crate. Instead throw little treats inside so he goes in on his own. Check on him often, and when he wakes up immediately take him outside to the area designated for him to relieve himself.

Figure 32: Puppies will find all kinds of places to rest during the day.

Once you've survived the first day, it'll be time for your first night with your puppy. The first night home with your new puppy can be a trying experience for all involved. The first time your puppy has spent the night away from his mother may result in some whining and crying. With a little preparation and patience, you can make the most of the first night with your puppy.

Before bedtime, take up any food or water after dinner to make sure your puppy is running on empty when it's time to sleep. Otherwise, you could be making trips to the bathroom during the night, or worse, your puppy will use the bathroom in the house. Just before you go to bed, take your puppy outside and wait for him to go. When he does praise him and bring him back inside.

Make sure your puppy gets in a little playtime before you go to bed. This will help make him to be tired enough to sleep through the night. Try to prevent him from napping before bedtime or else your puppy may be ready to play when you're ready to sleep.

You may decide to let your puppy sleep in your bedroom at night. The close contact throughout the night will help your puppy adjust to you and establish you as leader. Don't let the puppy sleep in the bed with you unless you are planning for him to sleep there in the future. He'll eventually expect to be allowed in bed. If you do choose to allow him to spend his night in your bedroom, you should put the crate in your room and use that to secure him while he sleeps.

If your puppy does wake up and or cry at night, you need to decide if he has to go to the bathroom or if he's looking for attention. If he's been quiet for a few hours and suddenly starts to cry or whine, he may need to be brought outside to relieve himself. Puppies have small bladders, so you'll likely have to take him out at least once during the night. A good rule of thumb is to add one to your puppy's age in months and that's generally how long he can go without going outside. A two-month-old puppy can wait three hours, so that means your puppy will probably need to go out at least twice over the course of the night.

If your puppy is crying and you're certain it's not because he needs to relieve himself, reach down and soothe him a little. Don't spend too much time soothing him though as this will only reinforce the behavior and he'll start to cry even more. If he continues to whine, give him a gentle but firm nudge and say "quiet" or shush him. If you are unable to stop him from crying you can choose to ignore him. Eventually your puppy will learn that crying at night gets him nowhere. The more consistent you are in your approach, the quicker the situation will be resolved.

In the morning, as soon as your puppy wakes up, carry him outside. Don't let him walk there or he may be tempted to go before he gets outside. When he's outside, wait as long as it takes for him to go. Then give him much praise.

As with any new baby, you may not get much sleep the first night with your new puppy. If you're patient and understanding, your puppy will learn what you expect of him when it's time to sleep. You both should wake up rested and ready for the day after a few nights together.

If possible, plan to be home with the puppy the first 3 to 4 days. Plan to keep the puppy involved with plenty of attention from children and other family members. Make a plan that when you are not with the puppy, he is sleeping. This will help speed up the housebreaking process. If you have young children who are not familiar with how to handle puppies, you should spend some time with them during these first few days explaining common sense rules on how to play with the puppy.

To have a successful journey through puppyhood, it helps to make a dog care schedule. This is especially helpful if you have children. It is also helpful to your puppy as he will get to know the other members of the family and get used to a routine. The members of the family will know what is expected of them. Decide who is responsible for which tasks and when they should be done each day.

Decide when the puppy will be fed and when the puppy will be walked. Scheduling bathroom breaks will help speed up the process and ensure that someone will do the job. Plan to spend at least twenty minutes per day exercising your dog. This will not only give them a healthy start, but one that is free of trouble. During your playtime, practice obedience training and basic commands. Get everyone involved that will be a part of the dog's life.

It is important at an early age to teach your children respect for dogs. Once your kids have been assigned their tasks and understand the basic rules of dog care, they should be taught how to treat dogs with respect. Make it clear that roughhousing, pulling, poking, smothering, and other such behavior can hurt your new pup or cause him to develop distrust – the one trait we greatly want to avoid. You can use a stuffed animal to explain to younger children how to pet and hold a puppy without traumatizing their new furry friend. Teach children to never grab an item from a dog. Dogs can be protective of their toys and may bite if you try to take them. We will be teaching our new puppy a command for releasing objects during our training sessions. Also, teach children to never bother a dog while they are sleeping or eating.

Even if you think your pet is the sweetest animal in the world, never leave a child unsupervised with a puppy or dog. Kids can be curious and may pull the dog's ears or poke at him if you're not around. Having your children and the dog in sight is not enough. Always be in a position to intervene immediately if anything happens, for the safety of your kids and the dog.

Once your new pup is acquainted with your family, it is time to introduce him to your other pets, if you have them. Dogs are pack animals with a hierarchy based on who is most dominant. One dog will lead and the others will follow in rank. If you're introducing a new puppy to your dog or other pets, he'll need to find his place in the pack.

Figure 33: Dogs are pack animals, one dog will lead and the others will fall in rank.
"Beag", "Obie" (a deerhound), and "Bramble", taken in 2014
at Kilcrea Castle, County Cork, Ireland.
Photograph used with permission by Liam O Shea.

It's best to introduce a new puppy to your adult dog in a place that's new to both of them. Because dogs are territorial by nature, you want them to meet on equal footing rather than on your original dog's home turf. If possible, have two people help out by handling your dog and puppy for you. Let them sniff around and check each other out while you talk to them softly. If you notice any aggressive behavior, distract the dogs and lead them away from each other. Let them cool off and introduce them again a little later.

It is not recommended that Patterdales be around other small furry pets. Cats, hamsters, guinea pigs, and the like are potential game animals for your Patterdale. As we've covered, Patterdales will chase anything that moves. One glance of a darting piece of fur and the hunt is on.

Your puppy is going to require regular visits to the veterinarian so you want to establish good habits from the start. You will want to visit your veterinarian shortly after you bring your puppy home. Most breeders require an immediate veterinary exam in order for any health guarantees to be valid. Schedule your puppy's first appointment as early in the morning as possible, preferably when the clinic opens or when there are fewer people. Since your puppy hasn't completed his vaccinations, he's susceptible to diseases. You don't want to expose him to other dogs in the waiting area.

During the veterinarian's examination keep your puppy calm and relaxed. Praise him softly during the exam and afterwards. Your puppy's first visit to the veterinarian will involve a basic health check and his first set of vaccinations. Your puppy will be weighed and given a thorough inspection to check his coat, ears, eyes, heart, lungs, teeth and gums. Bring along any health records or documentation you received from the breeder or rescue organization. This will give the vet knowledge of your puppy's previous care.

Once your puppy is settled in, you may want to enroll him in an obedience class. Not just for training, it is also helpful in getting your puppy socialized to other dogs. If all goes well the first round you may decide to go on to agility or competition classes. By planning ahead, you can set your puppy up for success and ensure a wonderful relationship for years to come. Setting expectations for the members of the household will make it an easy transition for them to be a meaningful part of your family.

Figure 34: "Voodoo", shown here at six months old, enjoys a warm March afternoon in Atlanta, GA.

"I feel about airplanes the way I feel about diets.
It seems to me that they are wonderful things for other people to go on."

Jean Kerr

Figure 35: "Milo", taken April 2014 in Northampton, Northamptonshire, UK.

[7]

Doggie Diet

WE LOVE and welcome the change of each new season in our house. The start of winter is always particularly exciting as the holiday season draws in and we dream of the possibility of snow (we live in Atlanta, Georgia and only get a good packing snow every couple years). Every season also brings with it special dishes we only serve at that particular time of year; for winter one of our favorites is fondue. There is nothing like staying in on a Saturday night, the family nestled in our pajamas, watching a holiday classic while dipping our food-laden fondue forks into a pool of boiling broth over an open flame.

One particularly frosty night we had primed for a wonderful feast. We had prepped a platter of broccoli, cauliflower, mushrooms and asparagus and set it on our coffee table. We had pulled out at least six different sauces including: grated horseradish, Dijon mustard, Chinese hot mustard, steak sauce, peanut sauce, and a spicy chili paste. We had splurged on peeled shrimp, scallops, filet mignon, and chicken. My daughter and husband were upstairs changing when I went to the kitchen to retrieve our fondue pot from the stove and move it to the Sterno burner in the living room. We all met in the den at the same time. My husband put the "Miracle on 34th Street" DVD into the player. Our favorite little terrier was lying four feet up at the end of the couch, drifting off into la-la-land. As we put our first skewers into the pot my husband asked if I had forgotten to put out the steak. I replied that I was certain I had. But, when I looked down at the serving platter of meat one section had disappeared. I had created triangles of each type on the round platter and one, and only one, was missing - the steak! No wonder our little friend was on his back - to help digest the pound of filet mignon his selective taste had deemed worthy of the risk of retribution.

You Are What You Eat

We aren't about to talk about the "D" word - are we? Yes, we are. But before your fingers do the running, vaulting pages to get to the next chapter, let us relax their pace. This is about your Patterdale Terrier's nutritional needs. It is not our intention to help you with your own diet (unless you have a particular fondness for kibble). Rest assured, there won't be any meal cards handed out during this session. We will not be detailing some complicated point system that requires the enslavement of a calculator to see if you can eat another spoonful of cottage cheese. No we will keep this simple.

The most important consideration when designing your doggie diet is a phrase my mother told me when my daughter first started eating solid food. She said, "You may not be able to control what goes into your mouth, but you can certainly control what goes into hers" (granted my mother used a stronger first generation immigrant vocabulary – but you get the point). Your dog can't feed himself. You have to provide for him. This means, you are responsible for making sure his nutritional needs are met so that he will grow into a healthy, happy, well-adjusted family member.

Don't worry; it's not all that hard. We bet you've been feeding yourself for years now and you're getting pretty good at it. So let's run through the basics of doggie diet design.

What do I feed my Patterdale Terrier?

When deciding what to feed your dog, there are three defined strategies with the opportunity to blend across the lines:
1. Commercial Dog Food
2. Raw Food
3. Home Cooking

What you feed him is largely based upon how close you want to be to his food. A good baseline may be how close you are to yours.

1. Commercial Dog Food

Are you the type of person who generally goes out to eat, picks out ready-made meals from the grocery store, or sticks to simple recipes? If so, you probably want to choose commercially prepared dog food. There is absolutely nothing wrong with this option. There are some good, quality diets out on the market today. The key to success is simply choosing a good dog food and not a bad one. The overwhelming majority of dog foods on the market are filled with grain fillers like corn or rice that are flavored to taste like meat. This is the doggie equivalent to junk food. While it does provide calories for your dog it certainly isn't the best nutritional source. Just because a label says nutritionally complete doesn't mean that it isn't just a sleeve of doggie French fries with a multi-vitamin sprinkled over the top. So how do you pick out a good, quality dog food? The easiest way is simply to go to an independent authoritative source. At the time of this publishing there are a couple great sources that meet our criteria: www.PetfoodRatings.net and www.DogFoodAnalysis.com (our personal favorite). These sites rate the quality of dog food based on the ingredient label. As some critical information is missing from the label (such as quantity of each ingredient) there is a little bit of guesswork in the analysis. But until more information is available these are your best resources for impartial reviews of dog food. If you reference the two sites you'll notice that top rated commercial diets are generally the same between the two.

Figure 36: "Voodoo", photograph taken in May 2010 in Atlanta, GA, USA.

Now another question you may ask is "Should I feed my dog wet or dry food?" We'll make this simple, why ask why – choose dry. We can't think of a single dog we've known that's grown up on wet food that hasn't had major dental issues in life, not to mention the choking breath that comes with it. Dry food has many advantages over wet food. One, dry food helps reduce tartar buildup. Two, dry food doesn't stink or spoil in your dog's dish. Three, dry food is easy to store and travel with. In short, unless there's a medical reason that your dog needs wet food - use dry.

Another nice feature of using dry food is the ability to feed your dog from kibble dispensing toys. We use the balls almost exclusively for our dogs. When we need to leave the house we put our canine children in the kitchen with full kibble balls. Voodoo and Rio push theirs around with their nose following after to lap up the food as it falls out. Carrabelle is even more resourceful as she just bats it around with her paw to get the kibble. The point is it gives them a job to do for their food.

O.K. so you've decided to use dry, you've gone to the sites and printed or written down some of the top rated dog kibble. Next pick up the phone and call your local pet stores and see which ones carry the brands you're interested in. Hopefully with a little diligence you'll find a convenient local store that carries a good quality dog food. If you aren't able to find a good dog kibble in your area you can order it online and have it shipped, or drive a little further and buy a few bags at a time and store them until use (keeping in mind freshness dates).

Another question we often hear is: "Once I find a good dog food do I stick to one variety or one brand or mix it up?" There are valid arguments that changing diets causes intestinal upset in your dog. This is usually a temporary condition due to needed changes in bacterial flora that live in your dog's intestine to help him digest his food. This one argument aside, variety is truly the spice of life and that goes for your canine companions too. We enjoy changing our dogs' commercial dog food base regularly. This means changing varieties within a brand and to other top rated dog food brands. We like to change because we want to ensure that our furry friend isn't getting any vitamin or mineral deficiencies, or more likely, excesses that can build up over time. No one can possibly be assured that any dog food either pre-prepared or homemade is 100% nutritionally complete. Furthermore, changing your dog's diet keeps him from becoming a picky eater, a significant bonus when you're out of town and unable to find his "normal" dog food in an unfamiliar location. But the biggest reason for changing his food regularly is to help deter against the development of allergies. Recent scientific study has shown that most allergies are not present from birth but instead develop over time through under or over exposure to a particular substance. Feeding a variety of different foods from a young age can prevent the development of allergies.

So if you're bag of chicken dog food is running out why not pick up a new bag where fish, beef, lamb, rabbit, duck, venison or bison is the main ingredient next time? To prevent against intestinal upset (which can manifest itself as loose stool, constipation, or vomiting) between food changes, make the switch gradual over the course of a week. Begin with adding a little of the new food with his old the first day and gradually increasing the proportion of new to old until you run out of the old food. If you should notice a potential allergic reaction like skin redness or excessively chewing or licking of his skin, discontinue feeding him this new dog food and switch back to his previous kibble.

Figure 37: "Brandy" is on a raw food diet. Photo taken in May 2014 in Ruskin, FL, USA. Used with permission by Anglo-American Patterdales.

2. Raw Food

Are you the kind of person that is much more in touch with what you put in your body? Do you generally pick organic foods from the market and absolutely refuse to eat fast food? Then you may be a candidate for self-preparation of your dog's diet. In the past decade there has been a major movement in the adoption of designing Biologically Appropriate Raw Food (BARF) diets, also known as the Bones and Raw Food diet. The concept behind BARF diets is that our furry friends have been programmed through evolution to eat raw foods similar to those eaten by their wild ancestors. BARF diet followers state their dogs reap many benefits from a natural diet such as: cleaner teeth, shinier, silky coats, healthier skin, better breath, more energy, higher muscle to fat ratio, brighter eyes, smaller, firmer, less smelly stools, and less overall health issues.

O.K. so you want to know a little more - "how is a BARF diet structured?" The largest proportion of your dog's meal under a BARF diet is raw meaty bones. These should make up about 60% of his diet. Raw meaty bones are cuts that contain approximately ½ meat and ½ bone. Some common examples are beef ribs and poultry backs, necks and wings. The key here is that the meat is served raw and on the bone. We personally recommend freezing any raw meat source before they are fed to your dog to kill most potentially harmful bacteria. Please make sure to thaw the meat thoroughly before feeding it to your Patterdale pal though to prevent splintering of the bones. We also recommend staying away from poultry leg bones because they can splinter. Our last request is to avoid utilizing raw pork products in your dog's diet (pork can carry trichinosis which is fairly resistant to freezing).

The next largest proportion of your dog's BARF regimen should be vegetables and fruits at 20%. Try to make sure some green leafy vegetables get it in the mix, but other than that, just have fun with it. We are always fans of adding variety to a diet when possible. The only rule: no onions (they cause hemolytic anemia in dogs). You can try spinach, beets, celery, cabbage, bell peppers, tomatoes, apples, blueberries, oranges, pears, mangoes, cauliflower, carrots, green beans, squash, zucchini, bananas, etc. The more variety of fruits and vegetables your dog eats the wider spectrum of nutrients he receives. Make sure fruit is ripe and then take all your ingredients and puree them in a food processor. We personally endorse staying away from canned fruits and veggies, if you can't use fresh – use frozen.

Organ meats come next on the list making up 10% of the BARF diet with common ingredients being livers, kidneys, tripe (green not bleached), hearts, and gizzards. Meat can also supplement the diet with ground beef, chicken, turkey, lamb, rabbit, venison, bison, or even whole fish. Once again with any meat we suggest freezing beforehand to kill most hidden harmful bacteria. Dairy food is also good for his diet. Yogurt or kefir adds good bacteria for bowel health. Eggs provide protein, vitamin A, and minerals and they do wonders for the coat and skin. Cottage cheese is also a nice addition. Finally on the list should be vitamin B complex, vitamin E, vitamin C, kelp, and alfalfa.

If this sounds like it's for you, we recommend picking up a good BARF diet book and get on your way! Dr. Billinghurst is the un-disputed expert for this particular nutritional regimen. We've added a sample diet for an active 12 pound Patterdale to help you along (please adjust amounts based on your dog's metabolism). This is a whole day's feeding. It should be split into two meals:

4 chicken necks for the raw meaty bone requirement, then the following all puréed together and served: 1 raw egg (or ¼ cup of plain yogurt or cottage cheese), 1 turkey heart, ½ teaspoon nutritional yeast, ½ cup veggies & fruit, ½ teaspoon flaxseed oil, ¼ teaspoon kelp, ¼ teaspoon alfalfa powder, 50 mg Vitamin C, 50 mg Vitamin E, ½ can sardines or mackerel (or some whole fresh fish).

3. Home Cooking

We love the sound of home cooking. We see visions of mama in her apron in front of the stove making a wonderful down home breakfast. When home cooking for your dog you have to keep in mind that cooking removes many nutrients from raw food. If you do feel more comfortable cooking for your Patterdale you could just look at the BARF menu and cook the raw meaty bone portion and meats before serving. We would leave the veggie mash uncooked if possible.

Now there's no law that's keeping you to one diet exclusively. There is the opportunity to blur between the lines. If you want the convenience of dry food with the silky smooth skin and extra spring in his step that the BARF diet provides you can split your meals. We generally feed our dogs a small BARF meal in the morning and a high quality dog kibble at night. This provides us with needed flexibility for those times when we take our dogs on vacation and want to just take a convenient bag of dry dog food to use on the trip. This leads to the next question.

How often do I feed my Patterdale Terrier?

Feed your adult dog twice a day: once in the morning and once at dinnertime. Puppies are the exception here and should also have a lunch course served.

Figure 38: "Oscar", photograph taken in 2014 in Merseyside, UK.
Photograph used with permission by Richie Hooton.

HOW DO I KNOW HOW MUCH TO FEED MY PATTERDALE?

This question can only be answered by watching your dog. Each dog has a different metabolism, we have one pup that eats and eats without gaining weight. We have an older dog whose metabolism has slowed significantly and can't eat as much as he used to without putting on pounds. You want to keep your dog on the lean side, so start with the recommendation on the dog kibble bag or the BARF diet you're using and adjust accordingly. A good test to see if your Patterdale is the appropriate weight is to feel your dog's sides for ribs. If you can't feel his rib cage he is probably over-weight. Conversely, if you can feel his ribs and they have only a very thin layer of skin over them he is probably underweight. If you can feel your dog's ribs but they have a slight padding he's probably just right. If your Patterdale doesn't have a weight issue then just leave the food bowl down for 15 or 20 min at each meal and then take it away. At that point the meal is over. If your terrier is being fed a few high quality meals coupled with regular exercise each day, he should have no problem maintaining a healthy weight.

"The first wealth is health"

Ralph Waldo Emerson

Figure 39: "Nogger", taken March 2014 in the forest of Wiblengen in Ulm, Germany.
Photograph used with permission by Ralph Rückert.

[8]

Grooming & Healthcare

TO BRING A DOG into your home is to commit to a living being that depends on you for care and maintenance. Like raising a child, you are responsible for his physical and mental health. Regular checkups and vaccinations are a requirement for your canine's longevity and well-being. Tasks such as keeping your dog's nails trimmed is something you will need to add to your "to do" list (although if you have a particularly active digger you may find he files his nails down just fine without you). Where to find good information can be challenging, especially if you are new to the world of pet ownership. Outlined in this chapter are the basics on various parasites, vaccinations, and grooming techniques that will assist you in the fundamentals of taking care of your new canine companion.

The section of this chapter that deals with diseases and ailments is intended to be a go-to-guide in the event that your dog experiences symptoms of illness. The disease descriptions and care suggestions listed in this chapter are not intended as a substitute for veterinary care. They are presented as an overview for you to deepen your knowledge on canine health topics. It is our sincere hope that your furry friend never contracts any of the maladies listed in this chapter.

GROOMING

One word that we like to use when describing Patterdales is primal. They are no-frills, tough-as-nails terriers interested in rough and tumble outdoor activities. Driven to hunt, dig, and play, our Pats can require a bit more basic maintenance than your average lap dog. While their coats are easy-care, their indomitable spirit can result in more than their share of cuts and scrapes to be tended. So let us begin with basic maintenance of this little scrappy ball of energy we call the Patterdale Terrier.

Figure 40: Patterdales require very little grooming for their coats,
particularly if they have a smooth coat as seen here on "Sahara".
Photograph taken in September 2014 in Atlanta, GA, USA.

COAT

For those of us with smooth or broken coated terriers the only coat care we need to worry about is the occasional brush down with a dense natural bristle brush or terrier pad. Brushing is great because it cleans and conditions your Pat's coat by pulling his natural body oils through his fur. If your Pat has a rough coat, you may decide to hand strip his coat in the warmer months to keep him cool and keep his shedding down. This is not quite as lascivious as the name implies. It is the process of removing the dead outer coat to allow for a new outer coat to grow in. The safest way to strip his coat is just use your fingers. Grab tiny little patches of hair between your thumb and forefinger and tug sharply with the grain. The dead, molting hair should come out easily. You can also utilize a terrier-stripping knife to help. This tool is essentially a butter knife with a dull-toothed edge. When using you simply put you thumb against the toothed edge with small patches of hair in between and tug. Be careful with a knife that you don't cut the living hair too or you will end up with a hole in his coat. Stripping your dog's coat is a time consuming process so don't feel like you have to do his entire coat in one sitting. Work one area at a time. For instance, you can start with his back and sides (a.k.a. the "saddle" region). On another day you can work his legs, then on another his neck. Keep sessions short and speak to your Patterdale in an upbeat tone to keep it fun.

As a general rule, you should only bathe your Pat when necessary. Over-bathing your little beast with shampoo can lead to dry skin. Often times a good brush down with a dense natural bristle brush or a terrier pad is a better option to a shampoo bath. Now of course, if your Patterdale is anything like ours and habitually finds objectionable scents to rub all over his body – then yes, for the sake of yourself and everyone he comes into contact with, please bathe him!

Getting your dog used to taking baths as a puppy will definitely help prepare him for future washes. Most dogs do not love baths, but starting them early and making it fun can make your life much easier going forward. You will be glad you did, when he comes in from the outdoors with the horrid stench of some dead carcass spread all over his coat. Don't be surprised to find him ecstatic when he is in this state and looking to you for an expected pat on his head and a hearty "good dog"!

If possible, close your bathroom door before getting started. Keeping him enclosed will prevent an escape that leaves your house filled with wet, dirty paw prints and muddy shaken water. Before putting your dog in the bath, make sure the water temperature is warm and not hot. When washing, be sure to cover all areas but avoid getting too close to his eyes. Make certain to rinse out all soap and have him thoroughly dry before allowing him to go back outdoors. Keep a towel next to the tub to make sure that you can wrap your dog up as soon as he exits the bath. When selecting a dog shampoo, keep in mind that for the most part they are all equally effective. A more expensive shampoo isn't necessarily better. It is best to use shampoos specifically designed for dogs instead of human shampoo. Human shampoos contain lots of chemicals that may irritate your dog's skin. If you are someone who travels with your dog, you may want to consider a dry shampoo. This type of shampoo doesn't require rinsing and is great for a dog on the go.

Teeth

If your Patterdale is like ours, he will chew on everything and anything he finds: sticks, hoses, stuffed animals, etc. Just the other day our Pat stole our daughters shin pads and darted in the yard – farewell shin pads! All of this chewing can have an impact on your dogs' teeth. But the big question is – should they be cleaned? This has been the topic of much debate over the years.

According to many specialists, there is no scientific evidence that having your pet's teeth professionally cleaned will provide any long-term benefits. Also, professional teeth cleaning requires your pet being put under general anesthesia, which is not completely safe for your furry friend.

By providing raw meaty bones (BARF diet), dental treats (Nylabones, Dental Greenies, etc.), and healthy dry dog food we can keep down the tartar on our Patterdale Terrier's teeth. In addition, we can brush his teeth regularly at home. If you are planning to clean your Pat's teeth, it is best to start this routine while he is still young. To brush your dog's teeth, you need a few things to get started. Below is a list of canine specific tools that are effective for doggie dental care:

- Tartar Control Toothpaste – just like humans, a dog's teeth will collect tartar that leads to plaque buildup.
- Dental Cleanser Solution – kills bacteria that lead to plaque and gum disease.
- Finger Toothbrush – designed specifically for dogs, these toothbrushes are much easier to get in your dogs' mouth than a typical handle toothbrush.

To get into a regular tooth brushing routine with your Pat, you will want to introduce the procedure slowly. By introducing these habits in a gentle, friendly way you will ensure success. Start by making sure that your dog is comfortable with having your finger in and around his mouth (this will also be beneficial later down the road if you plan to show your dog as judges inspect your dog's teeth and it will be expected that your dog be comfortable with it). Hold your dog's muzzle with one hand and stroke the muzzle with the other. Slowly work your way towards lifting the lips to expose the teeth. Do this for a few seconds at a time until your dog is comfortable with it. Reward your dog with a treat and some praise for his efforts.

Next, you want to get your dog used to different tastes, start with something yummy like beef broth. Dip your finger in the broth and let your dog lick it off. Slowly work on moving your finger over his teeth and gums. Repeat this for 15-30 seconds for several days. After each session, reward with a treat and praise. Eventually you will want to switch to toothpaste formulated for dogs, meat-flavored toothpaste is available to make this an easy transition.

Once your dog is comfortable with these steps you will want to start doing some actual cleaning. Instead of jumping straight to the toothbrush you may want to start with some gauze or dental pads. Wrap your finger in the gauze, wet the gauze and apply the paste. Slowly rub your dogs' teeth in a circular motion. Continue across all of the teeth that he will allow you to do and then take a break for the day and again, reward with a treat and praise.

Within a week or so, your dog may be ready for a real brush. Grab his toothbrush and apply some paste. Allow your dog to taste some of the toothpaste from your finger and then from the brush. While holding your dogs' head gently, apply to the gum line and work it in a circular motion. Start on one side of the mouth working to the back of the mouth. Focus on the outside of the teeth starting with the top row and then move to the bottom row of teeth. Repeat on the other side.

Chances are, the first time you try to do some real brushing your dog will grow impatient. You may want to start with a few front teeth, and gradually add teeth over time. Eventually, you will be able to brush his entire mouth. Remember, at the end of each brushing session to reward your dog's cooperation with a treat and praise. This will make the whole process seem more fun to your dog as he will have positive associations with these cleaning sessions. Once teeth brushings are an accepted part of his routine, each session should take only a few minutes.

NAILS

We cannot tell a lie, nail maintenance can be tricky. If you're not sure about how to do it or just feel uncomfortable in general, it is best to have your vet trim your dogs' nails. It is important to keep your dog's nails trimmed as nails that grow too long can cause the dog to have poor posture and even harm his feet. Now here's the good part: our Patterdales keep themselves occupied with running and digging activities. These behaviors generally keep our furry friend's nails worn down with little to no trimming necessary.

If you do need to trim your pet's nails, realize most dogs are not big fans of this activity. For an extreme example, we had a terrier that would defecate every time we trimmed his nails. It is best to get your pet used to this ritual while he is a puppy so he becomes familiar and comfortable with the procedure. Start by regularly playing with your dog's feet to get him comfortable with you touching them.

The key to a successful nail trimming is being careful not to cut through the core of the nail that contains the quick. This is the fleshy area that is within each toenail. This can be tricky with Patterdales as their nails are typically black. The first few times you trim nails, just trim a little bit, staying away from the quick if possible. If your dog has an unpleasant experience the first time it will be harder to trim them next time as he will begin to associate nail trimming with pain.

You will want to make sure you work in an area that is well lit to trim nails. You want to begin by removing small amounts of nail at a time. Pay attention as you trim to the small white dot in the center of the nail. As you remove more nail, you'll eventually see a red dot that is the beginning of the quick. This is the blood supply to the nail and you will want to stop trimming at this point. If you accidently cut the quick the bleeding can be stopped with nail clotting powder, cornstarch or some cotton applied with pressure to the end of the nail.

While nail trimming is not an easy task, it is an important one. The earlier in life you can start trimming your dogs' nails, the better. Whether you or your vet perform the nail clipping, it is important to keep his nails trim. The longer the nails get, the longer the nail quick within the nails will become which can lead to health problems later on.

EARS

For the most part, ear care for a Patterdale is fairly simple. Occasional cleanings with a damp cotton ball of mineral oil or hydrogen peroxide should avoid ear infections. Being able to identify the signs of an ear infection is important as an untreated ear infection can lead to the closing of the ear canal. Surgical reconstruction could become necessary in extreme cases.

If your dog has an ear infection he may shake his head and whine. Another symptom is a yeasty smell emanating from his ears. His ears may also exhibit black or yellow discharge. The ear may be hot and inflamed and be sensitive to the touch. Causes of ear infection include: foreign bodies in the ear canal, food allergies, parasites, excessive bathing, bacteria, and drug sensitivities.

If you suspect your dog has an ear infection, a quick flush of the ear with warm water or a wipe with a warm cotton ball may remove foreign objects from the ear. If this does not appear to help the situation you will need to see your vet as an antibiotic treatment may be needed to treat severe infection.

EYES

Eye maintenance is fairly easy with a Patterdale, particularly because of their short hair. However, it is important to make sure you keep your Pat out of situations where they may encounter eye trauma. Possible sources of eye trauma include exposure to dirt and other irritants as well as allowing your dog to hang his head out of a car window.

We were guilty of this until we knew better – letting your dog poke his head out of the car window. It seemed harmless and boy do they love it! Unfortunately, it can be very dangerous as particles in the air can fly into his eyes causing damage. Also, in many cases if the dog can fit his head out of the window he can probably fit his entire body, which may lead to him jumping out. It is best to keep your Patterdale crated while travelling by car.

Figure 41: "Iris", taken April 2014 in Curmont, France.
Photograph used with permission by Masson Jean.

As you know by now, Patterdales are consummate diggers. Therefore, at some point you will most likely find his head in a hole full of dirt. Be careful when you bathe him later on. When bathing your dog, particularly with flea shampoos and other chemical treatments, do not wash his head past his ears. Getting too close to the eye area can be dangerous. To clean his head take a wet cloth (without soap) and gently wipe over his head as if you were petting him. When cleaning the eyes start at the corner of the eye and move outward, gently wiping out any dirt that may remain there. And of course, be careful not to touch the eyes.

Occasionally inspecting your dogs' eyes is a good idea. If you notice the start of any cloudiness or inflammation it may be indicative of a health problem. Eyes should always appear clear and bright. The area around the eyeball should be white. If your dog has any tearing, cloudiness or discharge it could be a sign of a greater problem and you may want to schedule a visit to your vet to be sure. If your dogs' pupils are different sizes this may be a sign of a problem as well. Below is a list of the most common eye disorders that may be seen in dogs. If your dog has any of the symptoms associated with these disorders you should take him in to your veterinarian as soon as possible:

- GLAUCOMA – Clouded cornea and enlarged eye due to an increased pressure in the eyeball.
- ENTROPION – A rolling in of the eyelid causing discharge and tearing.
- CATARACT – The eye lens turns opaque. This can result in impaired vision and possibly blindness.
- PROGRESSIVE RETINAL ATROPHY – A genetic disorder caused by degeneration of the retinal tissue. Night blindness is often the first sign. Retinas are no longer able to adjust to see in dimmed light.

On a side note, in addition to a body filled with fleas and a belly filled with worms, our puppy Carrabelle (who we found on a highway in Florida) had a cherry eye. Dogs have a third eyelid located under their lower eyelid. When the tissue that anchors this eyelid becomes loose it pops out and becomes visible as a bulbous red mass in the corner of the eye. In cases such as ours surgery was necessary to correct the problem.

INTERNAL PARASITES

The majority of internal parasites outlined here are worms and single-celled organisms that may choose to take up residence in the intestines of our dogs. The most common worms are roundworms, hookworms, whipworms and tapeworms. There are also single-celled parasites such as Giardia. What all parasites have in common is the need for a home, or "host", to survive on. In many cases they are looking to either feed off of your Patterdale or to lay their eggs on him. The parasites make their home in your dog, usually at the expense of your pet's well-being.

ROUNDWORMS

Roundworms are the most common of all of worm parasites. Roundworms (also known as nematodes) are white or off-white and about 3 to 5 inches long. They find their home in the dog's intestines (typically, the small intestine) where they consume partially digested food. They can grow as large as 7 inches long. Roundworms produce eggs, which are ultimately released through your dog's feces.

Almost all puppies contract roundworm in utero through their mother's placenta or through drinking her milk. Dogs can also contract roundworms ingesting eggs found on feces or by ingesting an infected animal (such as a mouse). Once a dog swallows the eggs the roundworms hatch within a few hours within the intestine. In some cases, they proceed to pass through the intestinal wall and into the lymph nodes, the liver, then onto the heart and lungs. From the lungs they can grow and reach into the trachea and eventually the throat where they are swallowed and sent back to the intestines, starting the vicious cycle all over again.

Young puppies are the high-risk group for roundworms; heavy infestations can result in serious illness and potentially death. Puppies with severe outbreaks often display distended potbellies. Other symptoms may include: weakness, fatigue, dry hair, decreased appetite, vomiting, and diarrhea.

Mature dogs of 6 months or older develop antibodies against roundworms which prevent the nematodes from completing their life cycle. When this occurs, the roundworms will encyst themselves in the body tissue of the dog. The encysted larvae will lay dormant until pregnancy when they will migrate to the mammary glands and placenta to infect puppies.

If your dog has an active case of roundworms you may find a wiggly worm in his stool. Your vet can identify roundworms through a fecal float exam. A puppy should have a fecal float performed at least twice during his first year and once a year thereafter as an adult.

Fortunately, the treatment of roundworms is simple. There are many commercial de-wormers available (e.g. Nemex, Strongid). Puppies are customarily treated at 2, 4, 6 and 8 weeks of age for worms. After administration of the oral medication, worms will pass in the dog's stool.

To help prevent your dog from contracting roundworms keep the area your dog lives in clean and free of fecal matter. If possible, try and prevent your dog from picking up and/or ingesting small animals. Preventative heartworm medications such as Interceptor and Heartguard Plus also prevent roundworm infestation.

Roundworms can be harmful to humans too. As mentioned, roundworms accumulate around where dogs relieve themselves or in contaminated soil. Always make sure that your children avoid playing in the area where your dog does his business.

HOOKWORMS

Not visible to the human eye, the hookworm is a common parasite in dogs. They are either white or reddish brown and are only ¼ to ½ an inch long. They are very thin and thus they are very difficult to see. Hookworms use their teeth to attach themselves to the wall of a dog's intestine. Here they feed on the dogs blood and move to different feeding areas several times daily. The adults lay eggs that are released in the stool. The eggs hatch and then travel to find a host where they will either be ingested or burrow through the skin.

Most hookworms are transmitted from mother to puppy through lactation. Hookworm eggs are also passed from the stool and into the soil where they can hatch and become infective to other dogs or humans. The eggs can be ingested or they can burrow through skin to migrate to a place where they can feed. In dogs they remain in the intestine, but in humans they travel under the skin, a disease called cutaneous larval migrans (CLM) or "plumber's itch". Humans are not the intended host of this parasite, and the larvae are believed to not have the collagenase enzymes necessary to break through the basement membrane to invade the dermis.

Hookworms are one of the most detrimental of all worm parasites. As hookworms feed on your dog's blood by biting into the intestines they leave behind bleeding areas, which can result in anemia. By feeding on the blood of the host animal the hookworm can cause a deficiency of red blood cells.

Some symptoms of hookworm infestation are your dog's gums may appear pale, and he may show signs of weakness. In addition, his stool may be bloody and/or black and he may exhibit diarrhea.

Detection of hookworms can be difficult as the worms are able to firmly attach themselves to the intestinal wall. Diagnosis is best performed through a fecal float exam that reveals the eggs in the feces. Hookworms can be treated with prescription medication. Most available wormers kill the worms but not the eggs.

To prevent hookworms remember where they come from: soil, water, and dog feces. Make sure all fecal matter is promptly disposed of. Clean your yard and household floors daily if you experience an infection. If you tend to have vermin in your yard, be particularly diligent to keep them away as they can serve as a transport host of hookworms. Make sure to keep children out of areas where dogs relieve themselves and always wash your hands. Also keep an eye on your sandbox (if you have one) as neighborhood cats may frequent it for use as a litter box.

WHIPWORMS

Whipworms are another common parasite found in dogs. They get their name from their whip-like shape. They are white and are anywhere from a ½ and inch to 3 inches in length. The front of the worm is very thin and tapered (like a whip) and the back is very thick. Whipworms reside in the area between the small intestine and the large intestine called the cecum.

Whipworms are contracted when a dog ingests food or water contaminated with feces or soil that contains whipworm eggs. In most cases, the dog cleans himself, licking his coat or feet and ingests contaminated dirt. The eggs in the dirt live in the intestine where after several months they hatch and mature into adult whipworms. The adult worms then lay eggs that are passed in the feces. The adult worms attach themselves to the intestinal wall where they feed on the dog's blood.

Detection of whipworms is not easy, and dogs that are infected may show no symptoms. The infection is diagnosed through examination of the feces for eggs. The females do not produce eggs daily, and several fecal exams may be necessary to identify a whipworm contagion.

Symptoms of whipworms may include anemia, diarrhea, and/or weight loss. If your dog has blood in their stool this may also be a sign of whipworms. Generally, the blood loss is not enough to be life threatening but diarrhea containing blood can be a long-term problem.

Whipworms can be treated with a prescription medication from your vet. Whipworm prevention can be problematic as whipworms can live for years in soil, resisting extreme temperatures. If you are certain you have whipworms in your soil, you will need to replace the soil or pave the infected area. Routine fecal examinations can also be helpful in inhibiting the spread of whipworms. When cleaning areas containing feces always wear gloves and wash your hands.

TAPEWORMS

Tapeworms are long, flat, parasites that attach themselves to the inside of a dog's intestine. A tapeworm body has a head, neck and several segments. Each segment has its own reproductive organs and typically contains many eggs. Tapeworms can reach lengths of several yards long.

Dogs typically contract the worms from another "host" organism such as a flea (which is ingested by the dog). Flea larvae may eat fecal matter that contain tapeworm eggs. The eggs hatch inside of the flea, which in turn becomes ingested by the dog. Dogs can also contract tapeworms from small animals like mice and other vermin as well as larger animals like sheep.

Tapeworms are not highly harmful. They may cause your dog to lose weight or have a distended belly. Often times the dog will seem weak. He may eat large amounts of food without gaining any weight.

Tapeworms are diagnosed by finding the worm segments on a dog's behind or around where he sleeps. The worm segments are easily identified as they look like small pieces of rice. Most tapeworms do not produce symptoms other than this.

Treatment is simple and effective. A prescription from your vet, either orally or injected will cause the worms to dissolve and be released via your dog's stool. Prevention requires an ongoing flea treatment program. If your dog is regularly exposed to fleas, tapeworms are likely to return.

HEARTWORMS

Among the most damaging parasites a dog can contract, the heartworm is a small thread-like worm that can grow to be up to a foot long. Although they are called "heartworms" they actually tend to live more in the lung arteries.

Heartworms are only contracted to a dog by a mosquito infested with heartworm larvae. The eggs mature into worms approximately 7 months after an infected mosquito bites your dog. The heartworms then migrate to the heart and lungs to reproduce. Transmission of the infected larvae is typically limited to the warmer times of year, but since infestation takes so many months year-round preventative medication is recommended.

Symptoms of a heartworm infection are hard to detect and typically not seen until the eggs have matured. As heartworms invade the heart and lungs a dog may begin coughing. He may seem sluggish and retain water. In some cases a dog may faint or cough up blood. The more active your dog is the easier it will be to detect the heartworm infection.

Most dogs that contract heartworm will die if not properly treated. Treatment is delivered in the form of injections. The injections kill the adult heartworms in the blood vessels of the heart.

Prevention is very easy and can be achieved with a monthly medication either in a pill or topical form. Prevention in puppies should begin at 6-8 weeks of age. Every dog should take heartworm preventative medication.

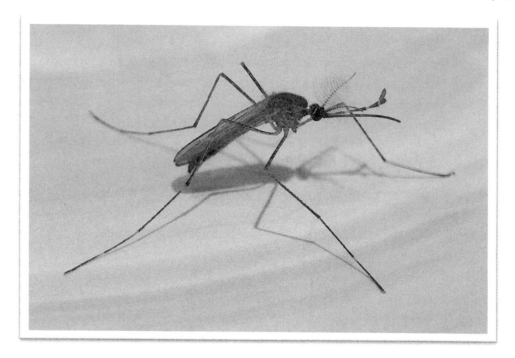

Figure 42: Heartworms are only contracted to a dog by a mosquito infested with heartworm larvae.
Photograph by Enrique Dans, 2007.
This work is licensed under a Creative Commons Attribution 3.0 United States License.

GIARDIA

Giardia are single-celled organisms that find their home in the intestine of dogs. There are many different species of Giardia and experts tend to disagree on which kind affect which types of animals. Infection by Giardia is known as Giardiasis. The organisms are pear-shaped and have a cartoon looking head that looks like it contains giant crossed-eyes, a nose and a mouth.

Ingesting the parasite in its cyst form infects a dog. The cysts are typically found in dirty or contaminated water. Once a dog ingests the cyst, it discharges a trophozite (a small organism with a whip-like tail). They attach to the intestinal wall and reproduce by dividing. Over time they form a wall around them and pass in the dog's feces, further contaminating the environment.

Giardiasis has very few symptoms. The most common is diarrhea, often mixed with blood or mucus. Dogs may lose weight without losing their appetite. Giardia are very small and do not pass with every bowel movement, aiding to the difficulty in detection. It may require several fecal tests over several days to diagnose a dog with Giardiasis.

There are prescription treatments available to treat Giardiasis. To prevent Giardia from spreading, always dispose of fecal matter promptly and keep areas clean where dogs have gone to the bathroom. Eliminate standing water or moist areas where the dog may play or sleep as they may ingest water contaminated with Giardia.

EXTERNAL PARASITES

Most every dog at some point in his life will come in contact with external parasites. These parasites often cause discomfort to our four-legged friends by irritating their skin. In addition, they can act as carriers for the transmission of internal parasites.

FLEAS

For almost everyone, the first parasites that come to mind are fleas. Fleas are the most common external parasites found on dogs. They are wingless insects that grow 2 to 8 millimeters long, slightly smaller than a sesame seed. While fleas are primarily viewed as an annoyance, they can also carry dangerous illnesses for both pets and people. The Bubonic Plague, while rare today, is transmitted through fleas. Cat Scratch Fever is another human-borne illness that can be transmitted from your pet's fleas. These diseases are spread because fleas are parasites that feed on the blood of animals.

You will most likely notice your dog has fleas if he begins to scratch and bite himself repeatedly. Interesting to note dogs do not itch due to a flea bite. It is actually the saliva in the flea's mouth that most dogs are allergic to that causes them to itch.

Fleas are large enough for you to see, but you won't always be able to find them on your pet, especially on our dark-coated Patterdales. The best way to check to see if your dog has fleas is to look for flea feces or "flea dirt", as it's called. To search for flea dirt, comb a section of your dog's hair. If black, dirt-like pieces are found, place them on a damp paper towel. If the flecks turn red, they are most likely flea dirt as the dirt contains your dog's blood.

Fleas can be troublesome pests to get rid of. They have a survivalist mentality and adults can live for upwards of two weeks without a host to feed on. In addition, pupae in the environment can remain viable for years. In order to control flea infestation you need to understand the lifecycle of a flea and attack them at all stages of their development.

Adult fleas are the parasites we see on our pets and in our carpets. Only 5% of the fleas in our environment are in the adult form. An adult female can only lay eggs when she has a food source to feed from, yes your furry friend! When feeding, the adult female flea lays about 20 eggs a day. These eggs are smooth, white and small – about the size of a grain of sand. The eggs quickly fall off your pet and onto the ground. For this reason, they tend to accumulate where your pet sleeps.

Eggs make up 50% of a typical flea population. Fleas eggs will hatch anywhere from a few days to a few weeks after they are laid. After hatching, they are in the larvae stage. Larvae make up approximately 35% of a flea population. Larvae are blind and have no legs. They move by two rows of bristles on either side of their body. They try and move into dark places and feed from flea dirt, skin cells, and other organic substances.

After two weeks or so the larvae form a silk cocoon around their bodies and enter the pupae stage. Pupae make up 10% of a flea population. While in the cocoon, the pupae mature into adult fleas. This process lasts one to two weeks. The adult fleas don't emerge from their cocoon until they sense conditions are right. They wait for vibrations or carbon dioxide levels to increase, signs that potential hosts are around. Without these signs adults can stay hibernating in their protective cocoons for months.

As you may conclude, in order to eradicate a flea population, you need to attack them at all stages of their lifecycle. Fleas can be attacked in your house by thorough vacuuming, washing of linens, and keeping your house clean. Additionally you can utilize flea powders and sprays in the areas your pet frequents. For fleas on your pet, you can utilize flea dips, powders, spot-on treatments, and ingestible pills to eradicate fleas. Flea pills are attractive as they actually get absorbed into your pet's bloodstream and kill adult fleas along with halting the development of their eggs. Another appealing thing about pills is that there is no insecticide being used in your house or on your pet. This is particularly nice if you have children.

TICKS

It's hard to talk about blood sucking parasites without bringing up ticks. Ticks are flat, eight-legged parasites that feed on the blood of their host. Ticks are no friends to our pets as they can harbor diseases that they then transmit. Maladies such as Lyme disease, Rocky Mountain spotted fever, tick paralysis, Ehrlichiosis, Babeiosis, hot spots, and skin infections are introduced from ticks. There are a number of different ticks, which will be happy to find a home on our canine friends. A few of the most common are: the American dog tick, the brown dog tick, and the deer tick.

The American dog tick (also known as the wood tick) can carry Rocky Mountain spotted fever and tularemia. They are widespread in the United States east of the Rocky Mountains and along the southern Pacific coast. These ticks hang on grasses and vegetation for an opportunity to attach themselves to mammals. While dogs are their preferred hosts they will also attach themselves to humans and other mammals. Adults are reddish brown with mottled white spots. The ticks turn gray when they are engorged with blood. After feeding for 1 to 2 weeks, a female tick will drop to the ground and lay over five thousand eggs.

The brown tick is another common variety. It is also called the "house" tick and is another carrier for Rocky Mountain spotted fever. These ticks are found throughout the world and while they favor dogs will attach themselves to humans or other mammals to feed.

The deer tick is also known as the black-legged tick. These ticks can transmit Lyme disease and Babeiosis. They are found mainly east of the Rocky Mountains. They are not picky about their hosts and will attach themselves to almost any warm-blooded mammal.

As with fleas the best defense against ticks is prevention. Many once a month topical flea medications will also work against ticks, as will many of the sprays, powders, and dips. Consult your veterinarian for product questions and recommendations.

Figure 43: Know what to look for when inspecting your Patterdale for ticks.
"Tick" by John Tann, 2011.
This work is licensed under a Creative Commons Attribution 3.0 United States License.

To keep tick populations out of your yard and home there are numerous sprays and foggers. If you take your dog for walks in forested and grassy areas it is wise to check his body regularly for unwanted hitchhikers. Most diseases transmitted via ticks take hours to communicate; so early detection is the key. Check all over your pet's body and pay particular attention to areas with little hair like behind the ears and in between toes. If you do find an attached tick use a pair of tweezers to pull the pest off at the point of attachment, or his head. Try not to squeeze the body of the tick as bacteria can be injected into your dog. Dispose of the tick by dropping it in alcohol or burning it. Once removed, clean the infected area on your dog with an antiseptic solution.

Ticks can also cause anemia in dogs if there is a significant loss of blood. Ticks can also cause "tick paralysis", a temporary condition that causes your dog to be paralyzed. Symptoms of a tick-borne disease include fever, weakened energy, and joint swelling.

MANGE MITES

Mange mites (also known as just "mange") can cause inflammation, itching, and hair loss of your dog's skin and coat. The term "mange" actually refers to a large enough number of mites to cause infection on a host. Mange generally develops on dogs with a weakened immune system. Invisible to the naked eye, Demodex mange is the most common form of mange mites found on our canine companions. In most cases, mange targets young dogs.

Almost all dogs have mites as they are passed from mother to pup at birth. In most cases the dog and mites live in relative harmony unless the immune system of your four-legged friend becomes weakened. Male and female mites mate on the surface of your dog's skin. The female then works her way into the skin to lay eggs that feed on the dog's blood serum. The burrowing into the skin through the hair follicles and oil glands causes damage. Both the female and male mites die shortly after the mating process is complete.

When a dog scratches the infected area, it becomes inflamed leading to dry skin and scabs. In serious cases blood serum will be seen bleeding from the lesions. If mange goes untreated it may cause death due to an elevated bacterial infection.

Mange is not contagious, and mites can live on both dogs and humans without ever being detected. Symptoms of a mite infection include irritated, itchy skin, hair loss, as well as cracked skin and scabs.

There are 3 forms of Demodicosis, or infection via Demodex mites. Localized Demodicosis occurs as scaly and/or bald patches on a dog's face. Treatment is not necessary; however, there are ointments and gels available to control the mites. The second form is generalized Demodicosis. In these cases, the entire body of the dog is covered with missing fur and infected skin. The bacterial infections make the dog very itchy and there may even be a foul odor present. Treatment of generalized Demodicosis includes avoidance of steroids, a flushing shampoo such as benzoyl peroxide, and antibiotics. Often when seen in an older dog, generalized Demodicosis is a sign of a greater ailment. The third form of Demodicosis is Pododermatitis, which is mange confined to the paws.

Younger dogs are often able to recover from mange. Any dog with signs of mange should seek a veterinarian consultation to determine the severity and for a customized treatment. Good nutrition, keeping up your dog's vaccinations, and control of parasites such as worms and fleas can help prevent the onset of mange in dogs.

RINGWORM

Ringworm is a common fungus that can affect a dog's skin and coat. The fungus goes by the scientific name Microsporum Canis. The ringworm fungus is transmitted by spores that can be passed from the hair of infected animals or the ground or toys with which they play. The spores invade the hair follicles where they grow and cause ringworm. Ringworms can be passed from pets to humans and vice versa. Most healthy dogs and people are not overly susceptible to ringworms and don't exhibit symptoms. Ringworm infections generally strike puppies or children.

The symptom of ringworm is a growing red ring on the skin with scaly skin and hair loss at the center. Secondary bacterial infections can cause itchy skin and scabs, and you may see your puppy scratching these areas. The ringworm virus prefers to live in hot and humid climates. Ringworm spores can live for long periods of time.

Most typically, ringworm scabs are found on the head but they can also show up on the feet, tail, and legs. A common quick means to determine if your pet has ringworm versus mange or some other skin ailment is to use ultra-violet light. Ringworm fungus will typically glow green under ultra-violet light. Definitive testing involves making a fungal culture from an infected hair sample.

Treatment involves using antifungal topical creams & lotions containing miconazole. This can be combined with shampoo treatments containing miconazole if there are several areas of infection. Treatments should continue for two weeks after the symptoms disappear.

There are no current vaccines for ringworm and the spores can remain viable for a year in the environment. To prevent infection, vacuum potentially infected carpets. Mop and wash hard surfaces along with toys and grooming equipment with a diluted bleach solution, 1:10 strength. Contaminated clothing and fabrics should be washed with bleach. As ringworms can be passed to humans, keep children and people with weakened immune systems away from pets exhibiting ringworm.

DISEASES & VACCINATIONS

Just like people, there are various diseases our dogs can come in contact with. And just like people there are vaccines available for our pets that can prevent diseases or reduce the illnesses they produce. Making sure your dog is current on vaccinations is one of the easiest ways to make sure he lives a long and happy life.

VACCINATIONS

It is important to vaccinate your Patterdale for both his health and the health of your human family. Vaccines are composed of inactivated virus organisms. When they are introduced into the body they cause the immune system to respond to fight the virus. In this way, if our pet is ever introduced to a live virus they have an immune system that will recognize and quickly fight the virus before it has a chance to propagate itself to dangerous levels in his body.

There are two main categories of vaccine: Core and Non-Core. Core vaccines are considered essential because of the severity of the disease these viruses produce or their ability to transmit to humans. The core vaccines are: canine parvovirus, distemper, canine hepatitis and rabies. Non-Core vaccines are generally administered to your pet based on the threat level of diseases found in your geographical area or areas you may visit with your pet. To understand the appropriate core and non-core vaccines for your dog you should talk to a veterinarian.

Many vaccines are administered via injections through your dog's skin, while others can be dispensed through your dog's nose in the form of a spray. Puppies are most at risk for diseases as they have immunes systems that are still weak. A typical puppy vaccination schedule should begin at 6 weeks of age, with three sets of vaccines delivered every 4 weeks. Adult vaccination booster vaccinations are generally recommended annually.

CANINE DISTEMPER

Closely related to human measles, canine distemper is a very serious viral disease that can attack the gastrointestinal, respiratory, and nervous system of your pet. It is much less common these days as most puppies receive vaccinations to prevent against it. Formerly being the number one killer of puppies, it is now a rare but fatal disease that should always be taken seriously if symptoms appear.

The disease is transmitted through the air via respiratory emissions of infected animals. The virus can also be spread through contact with urine. The virus enters the dog through the nose or mouth and begins to replicate. Within a day the virus spreads to the respiratory system. Canine distemper also affects other animals and contact with various animals such as raccoons and skunks can also cause the disease to be transmitted.

Distemper is often fatal. Puppies and older dogs that have not been vaccinated are at high risk. Irreversible damage can be caused to your dog's nervous system if he contracts distemper. Symptoms include a watery, pus-like discharge,. Other generic symptoms include lethargy, fever, and coughing. This can be coupled with a reduced appetite, vomiting, and diarrhea. In extreme cases the virus may attack the nervous system causing seizures and potentially paralysis. If your dog has any of the above-mentioned symptoms, take him to the veterinarian immediately.

Once contracted, there is no specific medication available to treat distemper. Antibiotic treatment is directed at the secondary infections. For a dog that has distemper, the typical protocol is to keep him clean and warm and encourage him to eat. As can be seen, the key to distemper is vaccination. Until your dog has received his vaccination it is best to keep him away from places where other dogs congregate.

PARVOVIRUS

Canine parvovirus, also known as "Parvo", is one of the most highly contagious and common viral diseases known to dogs. Parvovirus passes itself in the stool of infected animals. Oral contact with anything that has been contaminated with infected feces can pass the disease on to the next canine victim. The virus can survive on contaminated material for several months waiting for a new host. Parvovirus is highly resistant to disinfectants; a 1:30 bleach/water solution is the best-known cleaning agent. While Parvo can affect any age of dog, puppies six weeks to six months of age are the most susceptible. Infected puppies that are not provided appropriate treatment exhibit mortality rates as high as 80%.

Parvovirus once inside a host attacks rapidly, reproducing within tissue cells. Often these are the cells lining the gastrointestinal tract. Parvo can also attack white blood cells and the heart. It can destroy vital organs, making them non-functional.

The first symptoms of Parvo are weakness and depression. This is followed by foul smelling, bloody stool. Vomiting, loss of appetite, dehydration, and fever are other symptoms that Parvo victims can exhibit. Definitive detection can be achieved through blood or fecal testing.

Treatment of the disease is done primarily through hydrating the dog to replace fluids lost through vomiting and diarrhea. Without the proper amount of fluids, survival is unlikely. Blood transfusions may be necessary in extreme cases. Antibiotics are typically prescribed to prevent bacterial infection.

Once again, the best prevention is early vaccination (the first vaccination to transpire between six and eight weeks of age). If you have a puppy, keep him out of areas where other dogs frequent until he has received his vaccinations. When taking your puppy to his first visit to the vet, be sure to hold him or keep him in a travel kennel. Allowing him to walk around may put him in contact with other pets and contaminated material that may carry the virus.

BORDETELLA

Also known as "Kennel Cough", Bordetella is a highly contagious upper respiratory disease. Several different bacteria and viruses including the flu virus cause Bordetella. It affects the upper respiratory system of dogs and is analogous to the common cold in humans. As you might surmise, it is not overly harmful for healthy adult dogs. In these cases it is often just a bothersome cough. In immunocompromised dogs like puppies or older canines, Bordetella can be life-threatening leading to pneumonia and in some cases death.

Canine Bordetella is an airborne pathogen spread from one dog to another in the air. Areas that contain a high number of dogs like kennels and dog parks are common places to contract Bordetella.

The most common symptom of Bordetella is coughing. The dog may appear to vomit after the cough, as if something were lodged in its throat. Some have referred to the cough as a "honky" sounding cough. Other symptoms may include a watery runny nose, and in more serious cases weakened energy and fever. If your dog has been around other dogs or has been board at a kennel and has these symptoms it is quite possibly Bordetella.

Most dogs do not require treatment; however, antibiotics (to kill bacteria) or cough suppressants may be prescribed. If your dog has Bordetella it is recommended that your dog not use a neck collar as the pressure on the neck may make the condition worse. A dog with Bordetella should be isolated from other dogs until his condition improves.

The best way to avoid Bordetella is to avoid exposure to other dogs, especially if your dog is a puppy. An intranasal Bordetella vaccine is also a good preventative measure. If you are in a situation where you will be boarding your dog or putting him in places with lots of other dogs (like dog shows and races), you may want to consider vaccinating for Bordetella.

LEPTOSPIROSIS

Canine leptospirosis is caused by a number of species of spirochetes bacteria collectively known as Leptospira. Leptospira can infect humans, and many wild and domestic animals. The primary means of spreading the bacteria is through urine. Contaminated urine can make its way to a water source where it can remain viable for up to 6 months. Dogs can ingest the bacteria from drinking from a puddle or other infected standing water source. Working breeds, such as our Patterdale Terrier can come in contact with the bacteria if they spend a lot of time in woody or swampy areas.

Most dogs that have the disease show no symptoms. In those that do, fever and shivering are the most common symptoms of Leptospirosis. In more advanced cases lethargy, depression, refusal of food, vomiting, diarrhea and dehydration may occur. In truly severe cases, jaundice may follow, as the whites of a dog's eyes become yellow indicating hepatitis. Dog's that have ingested Leptospira can become carriers and shed bacteria in their urine for a year.

The primary target for Leptospirosis is the liver and kidneys of infected animals. Leptospira penetrates mucous membranes and moves into the blood stream where it begins to rapidly multiply. From the blood stream it will accumulate in the spleen, liver and kidneys.

Dogs that contract this disease typically recover within a week and become carriers. Unvaccinated puppies are at greatest risk for Leptospirosis and can suffer from life-threatening liver and kidney damage. Definitive diagnosis can be made through urine or blood tests.

Keeping your dog away from areas of standing water is the simplest means of prevention of this disease, as these are breeding grounds for the bacteria. There are also

Leptospirosis vaccines available if you live in an area where the concentration of these bacteria is high. As this disease can be spread to humans through infected water it is important to keep your home clean of the bacteria and keep a watchful eye on your children.

Infectious Canine Hepatitis

Infectious Canine Hepatitis is unrelated to the human strain of hepatitis. It is caused by a virus called canine adenovirus type 1 (CAV-1), which is closely related to the virus that causes Bordetella or "kennel cough".

Canine hepatitis is spread through the urine, blood, stool, saliva, or nasal discharge of an infected animal. It is taken into a new animal through the mouth or nose. From there, the virus enters the bloodstream and attacks the eyes, kidneys, and most notably the liver. Young puppies are most at risk for serious infections.

One of the first symptoms of hepatitis is fever. An elevated heartbeat may also be present, along with runny nose and eyes. As the disease progresses your dog may exhibit a loss of appetite, lethargy, coughing, vomiting, jaundice, and seizures.

Diagnosis is performed through a blood test for the virus. There is no specific treatment against the virus but rather toward the secondary symptoms. Treatment focuses on antibiotics and hydration. Blood transfusions are necessary in the most serious of cases.

The virus can be cleaned from your home with a bleach solution and other various disinfectants. Vaccination is the best form of prevention and the Infectious Canine Hepatitis vaccine is one of the core vaccinations for dogs.

Dogs that have recovered will continue to shed the virus for several months after recovery, so if you have other dogs it is important to keep areas where your infected dog has been clean.

Rabies

Rabies is certainly one of the most well-known and feared viruses of our canine friends. The virus Lyssavirus Rabies causes the rabies disease. Rabies is not a picky virus and will attack any mammal that becomes infected.

There is good reason that people have a fear of rabies, as untreated infections in any mammal almost invariably result in death. Rabies is normally passed through the bite of an infected animal or in some cases through its saliva. Once a dog contracts the virus, it spreads through the central nervous system and on to the brain. An infected animal will go through three stages. In the first stage, called the initial or "prodromal" stage, the dog will become shy and seek solitude. This stage can last anywhere from 2-3 days. From the first stage the dog may move on to the second or third phase. In the second phase, known as the "furious" stage, the dog becomes more restless and aggressive. He may tend to roam and become vicious. He may attack people and other objects without being provoked. In the third phase, known as the paralytic or "dumb" stage, the muscles of the throat be-come paralyzed and the dog will be unable to swallow. The dog may appear to be choking as it struggles to breathe. Regrettably, at this point the dog will only become weaker and die.

Diagnosis can be difficult, as dogs may show no signs until the disease has attacked his brain. Unfortunately by this point there is little hope for the dog's survival. It is recommended that infected animals be put down immediately if they have not been vaccinated. If a rabid animal bites your dog, his best chance is to quickly get vaccinated and quarantined.

While rabies is extremely deadly, cases of rabies have declined dramatically over the past years, as laws in most developed countries require rabies vaccination. Regular vaccination boosters for rabies are recommended over the course of your dog's life to insure that he does not become susceptible.

Lyme Disease

The Borrelia Burgdorferi bacterium causes Lyme disease. The bacteria is carried and transmitted by ticks, most notably the "Deer Tick". Lyme disease has the dubious distinction of being the most prevalent tick-borne infection in the United States.

The carriers of Borrelia Burgdorferi are usually rodents and birds. They carry the disease without contracting the illness. Tick larva will attach themselves to the rodent and feed off its blood. When the tick larva fully matures it looks for another host. If the tick attaches to your dog and transmits the bacteria, your pet can come down with Lyme disease. For a tick to transmit the bacteria it generally needs to be attached to your pet for 48 hours.

Most transmissions can be credited to the "Deer Tick". Smaller than the head of a pin, they are very difficult to see by doing a quick examination of your dog. Currently, most cases are found in wooded locations in the Northeast, upper Midwest (including much of Wisconsin and Minnesota), northern California, and the Pacific Northwest.

Lyme disease can be treated, and therefore is not a life-threatening illness if you are able to seek prompt medical attention. Indicators usually occur long after the tick has bitten. Once the disease has taken hold, symptoms include fever, joint swelling, limping, lethargy, and loss of appetite. A blood test can verify Lyme disease infection.

Treatment consists of antibiotics and is usually effective. Prevention of the disease is best done through tick control. Ticks can also carry other diseases so it is important that you keep them from biting your dog. There are topical insecticides available that have proven successful at repelling ticks. Avoid highly wooded areas where ticks are present to prevent your dog from encountering ticks. Insecticides are also available that you may employ for areas that your dog plays in.

Canine Parainfluenza Virus

The Canine Parainfluenza Virus (CPiV) typically causes mild respiratory tract infections. The main symptoms are coughing and a runny nasal discharge. Secondary symptoms may include lethargy and low-grade fever. While Parainfluenza infection by itself is not normally serious, the virus does damage to the lining of the trachea, which can lead to secondary infections. The resulting complications can lead to serious issues such as pneumonia and Kennel Cough.

Parainfluenza is transmitted through the nasal secretions of dogs that are carrying the disease. Infections are treated with antibiotics. Puppies are routinely vaccinated for Parainfluenza when they receive their "puppy shots", and are then generally given boosters on an annual basis.

To avoid Parainfluenza contagion, avoid kennels, clinics, and other facilities that do not require proof of vaccinations. Humidity and exposure to drafty areas can heighten the chance of your dog contracting the virus as well.

Coronavirus

Canine Coronavirus is a highly contagious virus that grows in the dog's small intestine and may cause gastrointestinal problems. It is transmitted when a dog ingests another dog's feces that has been infected with the virus. Coronavirus can be shed in the excrement of infected dogs for months after initial ingestion. It is mainly seen in dogs that are grouped together.

Symptoms of an infection usually include diarrhea, dehydration, and vomiting. To make a positive diagnosis, there are procedures for detecting the virus in fresh feces using electron microscopy. Coronavirus infection is rarely fatal. Most dogs recover without treatment. Puppies that contract the virus are at higher risk and may require antibiotics and intravenous fluids to combat dehydration. Most adult dogs have antibody to this disease from exposure to the virus. As Coronavirus is highly contagious, dogs that frequent kennels or participate in dog shows are at a high risk for contraction.

TYPICAL VACCINATION SCHEDULE

CORE VACCINES - recommended for all dogs based on exposure risk, severity of disease, and/or transmissibility to humans.
NON-CORE VACCINES - recommended based on a dog's exposure to risk.

DOG'S AGE	CORE VACCINES	NON-CORE VACCINES
6 to 8 weeks	Distemper, Measles, Parainfluenza	Bordatella
10 to 12 weeks	DHPP [Distemper, Hepatitis, Parainfluenza, & Parvovirus]	Coronavirus, Lyme disease, Leptospirosis, Bordatella
12 to 24 weeks	Rabies	
14 to 16 weeks	DHPP	Coronavirus, Lyme disease, Leptospirosis
12 to 16 months	Rabies, DHPP	Coronavirus, Lyme disease, Leptospirosis, Bordatella
Every 1 to 2 years	DHPP	Coronavirus, Lyme disease, Leptospirosis, Bordatella
Every 1 to 3 years (as required by law)	Rabies	

FIRST AID

Being the active, precocious, fearless little devils they are – our Patterdales may incur more than their fair share of injuries. The first aid mentioned here is geared toward identifying the type of injury and treatment options. If your pet is in a condition that makes you uncomfortable, it is best to get him to a veterinarian immediately. You may also wish to take a human first aid course, as many of the treatments prescribed to people can be adjusted for our canine companions.

FIRST AID KIT

Like the Boy Scout motto says: "Be prepared!" When the founder of the Boy Scouts, Baden-Powell, was asked what we needed to be prepared for, he replied "Why, for any old thing." Being equipped with the knowledge along with the tools you need to help apply aid to an injured dog is something we should take the time to do. You never know when you are going to need a first aid kit, so it is best to have one at the ready in the event that you do.

Our advice is to have one first aid kit for the home and one for travel. For our travel kit, we recommend a waterproof container to put your items in. With a permanent marker write the name and phone number of your vet, the nearest emergency animal hospital, and the number to a poison control hotline inside of the box. In your waterproof medical kit, include a Ziploc bag containing a copy of your dog's vaccination records and a picture of him in the event that he goes missing. So what else should we keep in our first aid kit? The following list is a good start:

TOOLS & SUPPLIES

- Scissors
- Nail clippers
- Tweezers (flat tip)
- Bulb syringe
- Small flashlight or penlight
- Thermometer (rectal)
- Cold/heat packs
- Sterile needle
- Eyedropper
- Tongue depressor
- Rubber gloves
- Disposable safety razor
- Clean Towels (at least 2)
- Paper towels
- Thermal blanket
- Matches

MEDICINES

- Wound disinfectant
- Antibiotic cream
- Antibiotic eye ointment
- Saline solution
- Anti-diarrheal medicine

- Cortisone spray or cream
- Nutritional supplement like Pedialyte
- Aspirin
- Hydrogen peroxide

Bandages, etc.

- Cotton balls
- Cotton swabs
- Sterile gauze
- First aid tape
- Non-stick pads
- Band-aids

Is My Dog in Shock?

Shock is the number one killer in dog accidents. Shock is very serious, and for that reason it is important that we be able to identify the signs of shock quickly. Quick diagnosis and treatment is the key to preventing death. If you have determined that your dog is in shock contact your vet immediately.

Shock can result from significant bleeding (internal or external), extreme illness, or dehydration. An injury may jolt the body into a state of "shock" by increasing the heart rate to keep the blood pressure from falling. The blood vessels that supply blood to the outside of the body narrow to conserve blood for the more important internal organs. The signs of shock include low body temperature, white or pale gums, a rapid heartbeat (more than 150 beats per minute) and rapid breathing. Your dog's legs and feet may feel cold and he will often appear lethargic.

If your dog is in shock, make sure to keep him as immobile as possible. Cover him with a blanket or towel to keep him warm. If possible, make sure that the dog's head is lower than the body. Make sure the airways are open. You may need to move the tongue to the side of the mouth so that it is not blocking the back of the throat. If your dog is bleeding, wrap the bleeding areas with gauze or towels and continue to apply wrapping to the area if necessary (do not keep removing dressings). And ultimately, rush him to an animal hospital.

DEHYDRATION

Dehydration in dogs can be instigated by diarrhea or vomiting, which causes an excessive loss of body fluids. It can also be caused by fever and overexposure to heat. Dehydration can become very serious and lead to organ failure and even death.

Symptoms of dehydration include dry gums, lack of skin elasticity, lack of urination, and tiredness. If you believe your dog is severely dehydrated and you cannot get him to drink water, take him to the vet immediately. Your vet will administer fluids intravenously or under the skin. You can try to administer Pedialyte (which is safe for dogs) but do not do this in place of seeking veterinary care.

HEATSTROKE

Also referred to as Hyperthermia, heatstroke occurs when the body cannot maintain a temperature in a safe range and overheats. Unlike humans that are able to sweat, dogs do not have effective cooling mechanisms and therefore can overheat easily.

The normal temperature of a dog is in the range of 100 to 102.5°F. A moderate heatstroke is considered as a body temperature from 104° to 106°F. Dogs can typically recover within an hour if given prompt care. A severe heatstroke occurs when the body temperature exceeds 106°F and can be deadly. Immediate veterinary assistance is required in the case of a severe heatstroke.

Symptoms that your dog may be having a heatstroke include rapid panting, pale gums, thick saliva, and vomiting. Some dogs may also experience diarrhea and shock. If you suspect your dog is suffering from a heatstroke, remove him from the source of heat immediately. Before taking him to your vet you will want to lower his body temperature by wetting him with cool water. You can also increase air movement around him with a fan. Do not use extremely cold water! Using very cold water can actually be harmful as cooling too rapidly can cause other life-threatening conditions. Take your dog's temperature with a rectal thermometer every 5 minutes. You will want to try to lower the body temperature to 103°F. At this point you will want to dry your dog thoroughly and cover him to maintain that body temperature. You do not want him to continue to lose heat. You will then want to take him to your vet as soon as possible. He should still be examined since he may have other complications that can't be detected. Provide as much water as your pet will willingly drink. Do not try to force-feed water. This may cause him to choke.

Most dogs will recover without any major health problems; however, severe heatstroke may cause organ damage. Once a dog has suffered from a heatstroke there is a good chance that it might happen again as their cooling mechanisms have proven to be inadequate. Steps must be taken to prevent heatstroke from happening again and avoid strenuous activities that take place on hot days.

To prevent a heatstroke, be sure to allow access to water at all times. If you will be outside with your dog and they will be active, you can fill a large bucket (depending on the size of your dog) or a baby pool filled with water. This is a great way to cool your dog down in hot temperatures and they will love it. If you can find a place that has shady areas for your dog to rest in that can also be helpful. <u>Never</u> leave your dog in a hot car, even for a few minutes. Beaches can be very hot areas as well. If you do frequent beaches, be sure to provide shade either via an umbrella or a tent. Dipping your dog in the ocean will help cool them off as well. If you have a dog that loves the ocean, you should not have a problem keeping them cool.

Figure 44: Dogs do love the beach, so be sure to keep them
cool with a dip in the ocean or under an umbrella.
"Voodoo" taken March 2012 in St, George Island, FL, USA.

Hypothermia

At the other end of the spectrum, hypothermia occurs when a dog's body temperature becomes too low for it to function normally. It causes a depression of the central nervous system, and may also affect heart and blood flow as well as weakening the immune system. Hypothermia is classified in three levels: mild, moderate, and severe. Mild hypothermia is classified as a body temperature of 90 to 99°F, moderate hypothermia at 82 to 90°F, and severe hypothermia is any temperature less than 82°F. Hypothermia typically strikes dogs that live in cold climates and have access to cold water and snow. Dogs that live outside in cold temperatures are obviously prone to hypothermia.

If your dog is experiencing hypothermia, he may be shivering and breathing slow. His heart rate may have dropped as well. He may have pale or bluish gums. You will want to check your dog's temperature with a rectal thermometer.

It is extremely important that a dog with hypothermia be warmed immediately otherwise he may become unresponsive and die. Your dog cannot warm himself and will need your help. You will want to warm him slowly with warm towels or blankets. If available, place the blankets in the dryer for a few minutes to warm them. Do not use extreme heat. If you have access to a hair dryer you can try employing this tool as long as it is on a low setting. If the condition does not appear too serious, you can also try a warm bath. Again, do not use extreme heat. While you are warming your pet call your vet to see what steps you should take next and if an office visit is necessary.

To prevent hypothermia, be sure to avoid extended exposure to cold temperatures. This is especially important for dogs that are either very young or old in age, that are smaller and thinner, or that have recently undergone any anesthesia and/or surgery.

BURNS

Burns on dogs are typically the result of an accident. Most burns are caused by heat or chemicals and can include getting too much sun or being too close to a hot object such as a stove or grill. Burns are serious injuries, and you should seek veterinary help immediately to avoid long-term damage as burns are very susceptible to infection.

Signs that your dog may be burned include missing hair, reddened skin, and blisters. Canine burns are classified like human burns, examining the depth and extent of the burn. Thermal burns are the most common and are a result of coming in contact with something hot such as hot liquids or fire. Chemical burns are less common and are typically the result of ingesting or touching a chemical such as bleach. Electrical burns are the most serious of burns and result from exposure to electrical wires. Puppies are susceptible to these types of burns, as they tend to chew on wires.

If your dog has been burned, you will want to cool the burn. Do not use ice packs as this might make the injury worse. Use cool water on the burn until you can get to the vet. Do not apply bandages, butter or Aloe Vera.

Diarrhea

Chances are at one point your furry friend will have diarrhea. Usually its nothing to be overly concerned about and clears up within a couple of days. If it doesn't clear up quickly, or is severe and uncontrollable, it can be a symptom of something serious and needs to be checked out. Puppies are of particular risk as they can dehydrate quickly.

Diarrhea is the quick movement of ingested substance through the intestine. This rapid movement results in one or more of the following symptoms: increased bowel movements, runny stools, or an increased quantity of stool.

Diarrhea can be caused by a variety of different things and determining the reason will determine the solution. Particularly true in puppies, parasites and viruses can cause diarrhea. Your vet can determine this by taking a stool sample. Both puppies and dogs can also get diarrhea from stress.

If your dog has additional symptoms such as prolonged diarrhea, black or tarry stools, vomiting, fever, or appears to be in pain, immediately call your veterinarian. They will want to know more about the frequency and appearance of the bowel movements. In most cases of diarrhea you will be advised to withhold food and administer small amounts of water for a day. A plain and small meal of meat and rice is often recommended afterwards. Once the diarrhea disappears, you can slowly change your dog back to his regular food. If conditions persist, you may need to change his diet completely. If a bacterium causes his diarrhea, an antibiotic may be prescribed. If he is severely dehydrated, intravenous fluids may be administered, as fluids ingested orally may not help soon enough.

Injuries and Fractures

If your dog becomes wounded you will want to be able to recognize what type of injury it is. This will help you determine what steps to take. Ligament and muscle tears are less serious than fractures, which need to be treated with extra care. If your dog has suffered from a fracture he will not be able to put any weight on the wounded area. If there is a complete fracture, the area may be completely limp.

LEG INJURIES

There are various types of leg injuries. You will want to make sure you have an accurate diagnosis from your veterinarian so that you know how to appropriately treat it. The most important factor to successfully healing a leg injury is rest. In addition, your vet may prescribe an anti-inflammatory to assist in the healing process. Leg injuries include:

- Sprains – the most common type of leg injury, sprains are caused by moving the leg in an unnatural way or overworking a joint. They are not life threatening, and tend to get better with rest in a couple of days.
- Dislocations – typically caused when the dog's leg is stuck somewhere while still moving. Dislocations are very painful and your dog will not be able to put any weight on his leg. In these cases, try and keep your dog's leg stable and get him to a vet.
- Ruptured Anterior Cruciate Ligament – another common injury, these are caused when the ligaments in their knees rupture by an abrupt twist. The twisting motion puts an abnormal amount of tension on the ligament and it tears. This typically occurs if the dog slips, makes a sudden turn while moving, or comes in contact with a car. Please get your Patterdale to a vet immediately, in this case.

PAW INJURIES

Unlike their human companions, dogs are barefoot for their entire life. Dogs are continuously exposed to a variety of different dangerous conditions, particularly if your dog likes to spend time outside. For these lovers of the great outdoors, paw injuries are common. If your dog has suffered a paw injury, he may limp and refuse to use the injured foot. He may also whine or show other symptoms that he is in pain. There are many different hazards that can cause a paw injury, some more obvious than others. Most canine paw injuries are relatively minor and will heal quickly with little help; however, some injuries are more serious and should be inspected by a veterinarian. If your dog has sustained a paw injury and you are unsure about how to treat it or if it is serious be sure to contact your vet. Paw injuries include:

- Cuts – minor cuts can be treated with antibacterial ointment and wrapped with a bandage. Of course, many Patterdales will simply remove the bandage and keep the wound clean with licking. Try to keep him out of the dirt until it heels

- Cracks – your dog may occasionally get dry cracked pads. In most cases simply applying some Bag Balm will suffice. Avoid human hand lotions as they will soften the pads, which is not what he needs. If the problem recurs regularly it would be worth consulting a vet.
- Lodged Items – Often pebbles, glass, burrs, etc. will become lodged in your Pat's paws, simply use tweezers to remove the item and then clean the area.

MUSCLE INJURIES

Muscular injuries deal with soft tissues that surround bones and joints. These tissues include muscle, tendon and ligaments. These tissues can rupture, tear, or bruise. Damage to these soft tissues may be debilitating, resulting in swelling and pain. Some muscle injuries can be treated with medication, while other more serious injuries may require surgery. Your vet will be able to examine your dog for swollen areas but x-rays may be needed to determine if the injury has affected the bone.

Mild injuries may be treated with anti-inflammatory medications and in most cases will heal in a few days. In more serious cases, a splint may be applied or surgery may be needed. Typically a vet will try an anti-inflammatory before considering surgery. If your dog's injury can be treated at home, make sure that you keep your dog in a confined area and keep him on a leash when he goes outside.

EYE INJURIES

Eye injuries include lacerations, scratches, proptosis (where the eye is forced from the socket), contact with chemicals, and foreign bodies (such as thorns or splinters) stuck in the eye.

Unfortunately, the tenacious spirit of your Patterdale can lead to an eye injury from his work in the brush and tussles with other animals. Eye injuries are not uncommon but should always be treated seriously. The key to preventing permanent damage is to seek veterinary care immediately. If your dog suffers an eye injury, make certain he does not rub eyes while you get him to the veterinarian. For these injuries often employing an Elizabethan collar is necessary.

FRACTURES

Fractures are caused by abnormal stress placed on a bone or set of bones. When the bone cannot endure the force placed on it, it will twist, bend, or shear causing a break. Fractures involving a joint are the most serious. Although most dog fractures occur in the leg; fractures can also occur to the skull, spine, ribs, wrist and pelvis. Pelvis injuries are typically the result of a major trauma such as being struck by a car. Fractures at the wrist and toes are common any may heal on their own without you ever knowing about it.

If you believe your dog has suffered a fracture, it is important to get them to a vet immediately as there may also be other internal organs that may have been injured. Your dog may go into shock, have difficulty breathing, or experience abdominal distention if internal organs have been injured. Often if your dog's leg is fractured, he may hold the leg up and/or not allow you to touch it. Fractures are classified as "open" or "closed" depending on whether or not the skin was broken or not. There are 4 types of fractures:

1. Closed Fractures – a closed fracture occurs when the bone itself is fractured but the skin overlying the bone is not broken.
2. Compound Fractures – a compound fracture occurs when the bone breaks and penetrates the skin. These can be dangerous in that the bone is exposed to external elements such as dirt and debris. Compound fractures are serious emergencies and should be treated as such.
3. Epiphyseal Fractures – mostly seen in younger dogs, these types of fractures occur in the growth plates that are located near the end of each bone. These growth areas, also known as "epiphyseal plates" are very soft and are more susceptible to fracture because they are weak.
4. Greenstick Fractures – These fractures result in cracks on the bone where the bone itself is not broken.

If you think that your dog has suffered a fracture make sure that he moves as little as possible. This might be difficult but try your best. Any pressure applied to the infected area will only make the injury worse and could cause further damage to internal organs. Move him using a blanket as a stretcher when possible. When necessary to pick him up, hold him with one arm under the fore legs and one under the back legs.

Treatment of fractures depends on the physical status of the dog. Several factors will play into the prescribed treatment of your dog. Your vet will take into consideration your dogs' age, the fracture type and location, and the normal activity level of your dog.

Your vet may apply a splint or bandage. If your vet chooses this as treatment, you will want to make sure that the bandaged area is always kept clean and dry. If surgery is necessary your vet may implant pins, screws, plates or wires. The intent of the surgery is to insure that the dog returns to normal function.

In the unfortunate case that a piece of bone has been sheared off, wash it off and place it in a container to take to the vet. A broken bone may never heal, despite the best medical care. Although many fractures can be treated allowing the dog to return to a normal and active life, in some cases the bone will never be completely the same.

BANDAGING

Knowing the basics of bandaging your dog can come in helpful if you are in a situation where you cannot seek medical treatment or it will be a while before you can. If you are not certain whether or not you should bandage your dog and you can seek medical treatment, always do. It is always better to have a trained expert look at your wounded dog. You may however find yourself in a situation where a little bit of knowledge can be helpful. There are several types of bandages:

- Head – head bandages are typically applied to stop bleeding from the ears. To make a head bandage, use strips of gauze or torn pieces of cloth. Wrap the cloth completely around the head, pinning the ears down. Be careful not to wrap too tight and cut off breathing. To make sure the bandage is not too tight see if you can place two fingers underneath the bandage. Never cover your dog's eyes. Once the bandage is in place, tape down the edges.

- Leg – you will want to consider using a leg bandage if your dog has suffered from a fracture or is bleeding uncontrollably. If your dog has an open wound try to cover it with a gauze pad. Start by layering several times with cotton. Next, place several layers of gauze over the cotton. The bandage should be snug but not so tight as to cut off circulation. Lastly, apply an elastic bandage or adhesive tape to keep the bandage in place. If his toes become swollen or cold remove the bandage.

- Splint – If your dog has a fractured bone, a splint will help immobilize the wounded area so your dog can heal. A splint will add extra support to the area below the elbow. Unless you know what you are doing, splints are best used on the front legs only. Placing the rear legs in a straight alignment can be detrimental.

ABSCESSES

An abscess is a lump that contains pus. Varying in size and severity, abscesses in dogs are often caused by fighting with other animals. Once sharp teeth or claws puncture your pet's skin, bacteria can be introduced which can lead to infection.

Abscesses are usually caused by foreign material getting under the skin. Bacteria and parasites may be the cause. The pus that is present is caused by white blood cells sent by the immune system to fight the foreign bacteria. As time goes by, the pus packet thins and eventually ruptures.

An abscess is typically characterized by swelling and redness of the infected area. Increased temperature of the infected area may be present as well. It is best to have your vet examine an abscess to evaluate the severity of the infected area. If the abscess does not eventually drain on its own, the abscess may need to be lanced. Treatment is aimed at helping the immune system fight off the infection. Applying a warm compress for 5 to 10 minutes a day, 3 or 4 times will help increase blood flow to the infected area.

Once the abscess has ruptured, a thorough cleaning with a disinfectant solution, such as povidone iodine, is usually recommended. You can also use warm water to clean the area. It is important to not allow your dog to lick the infected area as saliva contains bacteria that can be harmful to the abscess. If you are not able to prevent your dog from licking the infected area, you may want to consider an Elizabethan collar.

POISONS

First and foremost, always keep the number to a poison control center handy. If you believe your dog has ingested something poisonous, you will want to get him to a veterinarian immediately. Signs of poisoning may show up a day or two later so it is best to treat the dog right away just in case. If you can't reach the vet or get to one immediately, call a poison control hotline to receive assistance from a trained professional who can walk you through appropriate steps.

In some cases you will be advised to induce vomiting. It is always best to induce vomiting under the supervision of a vet, but sometimes you may not be able to get to one right away. In many cases you can prevent internal chemical damage to your dog by inducing vomiting before ingestion. Items that you may be instructed to induce vomiting for are: arsenic (found in rodenticides), chocolate, insecticides, weed killers, strychnine, shoe polish, shampoo, medications, and poisonous plants (see below).

If you must induce vomiting in a dog, give the dog hydrogen peroxide (3% USP) by mouth using a bulb syringe. Use one teaspoon per 5 pounds of weight. Before giving the peroxide, give the dog a little bit of food to bring up with the poison. Pull the lips away from the side of the mouth (forming a pocket) and deposit the liquid in the pocket. Do not pour the peroxide down the dogs' throat. If the dog has not vomited after 15 minutes you may try to administer the peroxide a second time.

Do not induce vomiting if the dog is convulsing, lethargic, unconscious, or in shock. Do not induce vomiting if the dog ingested acidic products such as drain cleaner and paint thinner. Corrosive poisons such as this can burn the throat on the way back up. You should also not induce vomiting for sharp objects such as bones, and petroleum products such as gasoline and lighter fluid. If your pet has ingested a corrosive you may be instructed to feed him milk to dilute the corrosive in the stomach.

If you know your dog has ingested an acid you will likely be told to rinse out his mouth. Then, using a bulb syringe aimed at the back of the dog's mouth, administer either Milk of Magnesia or Pepto Bismol (2 teaspoons per 5 pounds of body weight). This will help neutralize the poison and reduce damaging burns.

Here is a list of items poisonous to dogs:
- Human medications
- Rodenticides
- Household cleaners
- Garden/Yard products such as pool chemicals, fertilizer, etc.
- Human foodstuffs like alcohol (alcoholic beverages as well as ethanol, methanol, and isopropyl), almonds, apple seeds, apricots, avocado, cherry pits, chocolate, caffeine (coffee grinds, beans, tea), figs, garlic, grapes, hops, macadamia nuts, milk, molded food, mushrooms, nutmeg, onions, peaches, pear seeds, plum seeds, potato, raisins, rhubarb, tomatoes, walnut hulls, yeast dough. Sugar free items that contain Xylitol may cause liver failure and may even cause death in dogs. Even a small amount of Xylitol can trigger a significant insulin release that can be fatal in that it drops their blood sugar level to a dangerously low level. Xylitol is most commonly found in baked goods, sugar free candies and gum.
- Plants: the most severely poisonous plants include lilies, marijuana, sago palm, tulips, narcissus, azalea, rhododendron, oleander, castor bean, cyclamen, kalanchoe, yew, amaryllis, autumn crocus, chrysanthemum, English ivy,

peace lily, pothos, and schefflera. The list below catalogs most of the plants and foods known to be poisonous to dogs. This list is not all-inclusive and if you have a question about whether or not an item is toxic to your dog always consult your vet. The items marked with an asterisk are particularly fatal and should be treated accordingly.

- Almonds*
- Amaryllis bulb*
- Andromeda
- Anthuriaum*
- Apple seeds
- Apricot*
- Arrowgrass
- Autumn crocus *
- Avocado -leaves, seeds, stem, and skin*
- Azalea
- Begonia*
- Bird of Paradise
- Bittersweet
- Bleeding heart*
- Boxwood
- Bracken fern
- Buckeye
- Buttercup
- Caffeine
- Caladium*
- Calla lily*
- Castor bean or castor oil plant*
- Cherry pits
- Cherry Chinese sacred or heavenly bamboo*
- Chocolate Choke cherry, unripe berries*
- Crown of Thorns
- Chrysanthemum
- Clematis
- Crocus bulb
- Croton
- Daffodil

- Daphne
- Delphinium, larkspur, monkshood*
- Dieffenbachia
- Dumb cane (Dieffenbachia)*
- Elderberry, unripe berries*
- Elephant Ear
- English ivy
- Fig
- Four-o'clocks
- Foxglove (Digitalis)*
- Garlic*
- Grapes/raisins*
- Hemlock
- Hyacinth bulbs
- Hydrangea*
- Holly berries
- Iris corms
- Jack-in-the-pulpit*
- Lantana*
- Larkspur
- Jasmine
- Jerusalem Cherry, Winter Cherry
- Jimsonweed*
- Kalanchoe*
- Laurel
- Lily (bulbs of most species)
- Lily (Easter Lily, Tiger Lily)
- Lily-of-the-Valley*
- Locoweed
- Lupine species
- Marigold
- Marijuana or Hemp
- Milkweed*
- Mistletoe berries*
- Monkshood
- Morning Glory*

- Mostera, aka Split-Leaf Philodendron or Swiss Cheese Plant
- Mountain laurel
- Mushrooms & Toadstools
- Narcissus, daffodil
- Nettles
- Nightshade
- Nutmeg
- Pear seeds
- Pencil cactus/plant*
- Periwinkle
- Oak*
- Oleander*
- Onions*
- Peaches*
- Peyote
- Philodendron *
- Plum pit/seed
- Poinsettia
- Poison Ivy
- Potato (leaves & stem, peelings, unripe green potatoes)
- Privet
- Rhododendron
- Rhubarb leaves*
- Rosary Pea
- Scheffelera *
- Shamrock (Oxalis sp.)*
- Skunk Cabbage
- Snow-on-the-Mountain
- Tobacco
- Tomatoes (leaves & stem, green tomatoes)
- Tulip
- Walnut hulls
- Water Arum
- Wisteria
- Yew*

WOUNDS AND WOUND CARE

Dogs enjoy exploring and their noses will lead them to all types of adventures. They will find other dogs, other animals and countless other things that may end up being harmful to their bodies. With the exception of bites and puncture wounds, it is possible to treat some cuts and wounds at home. The general rule is that if the cut is smaller than half an inch you shouldn't need to see a vet.

Open wounds should be treated immediately whether they are bleeding or not. Open wounds are highly susceptible to contamination and will become infected if not properly cleaned and closed. Open wounds are typically the result of fights, attacks, and accidents. Different wound classifications are listed below:

- Abrasions – characterized in that they do not completely break the skin. Abrasions may or may not bleed depending on the severity. Indications of an abrasion include red, irritated skin. The skin may be bruised and/or embedded with dirt.
- Puncture wounds – usually caused by bites and foreign objects penetrating the skin. Typically small in size, a puncture wound breaks the skin and pushes into the tissue below. Although small, they should not be overlooked as they may become infected and form an abscess. Another animal's teeth, nails or thorns are often responsible for punctures. After the foreign object is removed from the skin, bacteria may be left behind under the skin, which could later form an abscess. If this occurs, your dog may run a fever and become lethargic. Eventually an abscess will drain but this could take several weeks. Antibiotics are often prescribed to prevent against and treat abscesses.
- Lacerations – occur when the skin is cut or torn. Lacerations can occur just about anywhere on your dog and be roughly any size. Common causes of lacerations include fights or attacks with other animals, jumping/climbing over or under fences, and contact with glass. Lacerations tend to bleed profusely.
- Avulsions – occur when a piece of tissue is torn away from the body. Most common avulsions involve part or all of the claw or toe of the dog in an encounter with another dog or car. Avulsions are not life threatening in most cases but they will cause a good bit of bleeding.
- Degloving – these types of wounds involve stripping skin from the body. In many cases the dog's tail or leg will get caught in something like a door or fence. With the protective skin layer gone, open tissue can be exposed to bacteria and therefore these injuries can be dangerous.

- Shot wounds – gunshot wounds are the most common type of projectile injury. Most seen in the thoracic and abdominal cavity, dogs that have been shot will go through some form of shock. Their gums may become pale and they may become lethargic. Whether or not you witnessed the shooting you will want to take your dog to the vet for an x-ray to determine the damage level.

- Bites – if your dog is bit, clean the wound and treat with a topical antibiotic. Wrap the wound and continue to check for signs of infection. If your dog was bit by another dog and you are able to talk to the owner, verify that their dog is up to date on their shots and if not head immediately to the vet.

- Snakebites - if a snake bit your dog, try to identify the snake. If your dog has killed the snake, take the dead serpent to the vet with you. The most common poisonous snakes in the United States are rattlesnakes, copperheads, cotton-mouth moccasins and coral snakes. The potential for death will depend on the species of snakes in your area. In the case of a poisonous snakebite, try to prevent your pet from moving. This will help prevent the venom from spreading further through the body. Do not apply a tourniquet or ice. Do not attempt to suck the venom out. Get to your vet immediately. Your dog will need to be observed for several days to gauge the severity of the bite and the amount of venom released into the dog.

- Insect bites – various insect stings and bites may cause severe reactions. If you witness swelling, disorientation, or difficulty breathing or moving get your Patterdale to the vet immediately. Your dog may seem fine at first; continue to watch him for a day or so for any unusual symptoms. If a hornet or bee stings your dog, you will want to remove the stinger. Scrape (with a credit card or similar object) the stinger away from the infected area, as to not inject more poison into the dog's body. Bathing the infected area in a baking soda and water solution can help relieve itchiness. You can also try calamine lotion dabbed on to the affected area with a cotton ball. An ice pack may be utilized to reduce swelling. If your dog exhibits symptoms such as shivering and/or vomiting, or a red and swollen bite is present, your dog may have been bitten by a poisonous spider. You should get your dog to a vet immediately in this case.

TREATING WOUNDS

First, clean the wound. In addition, you will want to make sure that there is no hair in the wound. You can do this by either using scissors or clippers to trim the hair around the injury. Flush the wound with warm salty water or a balanced saline solution. You can mix one teaspoon of salt with two cups of water or just use plain warm water if you do not have any salt handy. Do your best to remove all dirt from the wound. Removing all of the dirt will help it heal faster and avoid infection. If there are pieces that are hard to remove you may want to try using tweezers to remove them.

Second, control bleeding. This can be accomplished by applying pressure with a clean piece of fabric such as gauze or a towel. Additionally, you can try to elevate the wound to stop the flow of blood as well.

Third, medicate the wound. Apply a topical antibiotic cream (such as Neosporin), and reapply several times a day. If your dog will not leave his wound alone you may want to consider putting an Elizabethan collar on him until the affected area heals.

When your dog suffers a wound, it will be up to you to decide whether or not you should go to the vet. Only you can make this decision, and if you are not certain of what to do it is always best to play it safe and have the veterinarian examine him.

If your dog has suffered shock or appears to be in shock, or if your dog has a wound that does not stop bleeding within 15 minutes you should see a veterinarian. In addition, if the wound contains foreign material, appears to require stitches, or is the result of contact with a car or a large animal, head to the vet.

CHOKING

Dogs love to chew on things and are always putting things in their mouths. Knowing the symptoms to watch for and how to treat a choking dog could save your pet's life. If you believe that your Patterdale is choking, call your vet immediately. They will either walk you through how to treat your dog or ask you to come in immediately. If you cannot reach your regular vet, try to find the number of a 24-hour animal emergency center.

Symptoms that your dog may be choking include pawing at the mouth, consistent coughing, drooling or gagging. If your dog is choking he may also be vomiting and his lips may turn blue or white.

If your dog is capable of coughing, they may be able to dislodge the item that is blocking their throat. If they are not able to cough, you need to help your dog. Try to look in your dogs' mouth, moving the tongue to the side if necessary. You may want to use a flashlight to look in the back of the throat. Unless you can see the object, do not pull anything out. Dogs have small bones in their neck that could be confused for the obstruction. If you can locate the obstruction, pull it out gently with pliers. You can also try to hold the dog upside down and use gravity to help make the object fall out.

CONCLUSION

We certainly hope that your Patterdale Terrier will never need any of the healthcare tips mentioned in the chapter. But having had our fair share of terriers, and knowing the trouble they can get themselves into, we know how important it is to be prepared.

"If you get to thinking you're a person of some influence,
try ordering somebody else's dog around"

Will Rogers

Figure 45: "Beag", taken near Torc Mountain in County Kerry, Ireland.
Photograph used with permission by Liam O Shea.

[9]

Basic Training

IT WAS a dark and rainy Monday night at our local dog training facility. We had enrolled our newest rescue, Carrabelle, into beginner obedience. The only class that worked for my schedule was Monday night; the night when at the end of the day you just want to go home, put your feet up, and turn on the tube. Although I rarely looked forward to this 7pm Monday night class, I always left it feeling a wonderful sense of accomplishment - with the exception of this one particular night.

It had been a very wet day. The kind of day where rain refused to give up its hold on the sky and the sun never made an appearance. Though I had let Carrabelle outside numerous times that day; each time she sat under the overhang on the porch, staring back at me as though she was being punished. As you may be aware, many dogs don't like to go do their business in the rain. Being one of these finicky dogs, she refused all day and I really didn't think much of it. The day came to a close and at 6:30pm, Carrabelle and I headed out into the monsoon to attend obedience class as planned.

Class began as usual and as we were in the early stages of the course we were still working on the first and most basic command of "sit". The class started practicing commands with our dogs. At one point, when I asked Carrabelle to sit, she certainly did - to relieve herself on the carpeted floor of the facilities. Although a little embarrassed, this was something that happened before many times by other classmates so I quickly grabbed the cleaning supplies and took care of it.

As the class went on, she relieved herself a second time and then a third and fourth. The teacher, who was getting frustrated as well, asked me to take my dog outside. I knew it was pointless; we walked out back to the alley behind the building. As it was still raining, Carrabelle gave me that same sad look as if she was being punished.

131

I am sure she was thinking, "Why won't you just let me go inside?" Nonetheless, she was not going to take care of any business in that rain-soaked alley and we both knew it. We lingered in the showery backstreet for a few more minutes to make it appear as though we were at least trying.

I headed back inside and decided to give it another go. I imagined her bowels would be quite empty by now anyway. I assumed incorrectly. We weren't inside for more than a few minutes when she relieved herself yet again. At this point, I was seriously losing my cool. I cleaned up the mess and stormed out of the class. I wanted to yell and scream and cry in frustration at this dog. We got in the car and drove home. Me, angry as the night's storms, and Carrabelle as happy as a clam that she had relieved herself five times that night. I learned an important lesson that evening about training: always make sure both you and your dog are in the right physical and emotional frame of mind before trying any kind of coursework!

POSITIVE ATTITUDE

As a dog-loving family, we have experienced our fair share of training ups and downs over the years with our four-legged family members. There are a few things we keep in mind when running through obedience lessons. First, it can be a very physically and mentally challenging event for your dog. He won't always be in the mood to comply with your commands regardless of your energy level and treat allowance. It can also be an emotionally taxing event for you, if you are not in the mood to be patient and have a positive attitude. On the encouraging side, it can be a very rewarding and special bonding time for you and your dog. Mastering a command is a proud moment that may send you flying high on the success of communicating with your canine. Just keep in mind during your training journey that the most important key to success is to keep it fun.

Let's face it, training your dog takes patience and time. You need to be ready to lend both of these to your training efforts. Don't begin training if you are half-hearted about it. You don't want a partially obedient dog. You want the full package! Once you have committed to training, there are a few things to consider before starting.

Chances are you will be using some form of treat, whether it is pre-packaged dog treats, tiny slivers of cheese, pieces of hot dog, or a favorite toy. If you are training with treats it is easier to do so if your dog is hungry. Many dog trainers will advise you not to feed your dog until after obedience work. Also, keep in mind that better treats generally yield better results for those hard-to-train commands. As a general rule, the more the dog wants the treat, the harder he will work for it. We tend to use tiny pieces of cheese or hot dog for our training lessons.

When you are training with treats, always praise your dog while giving him a treat. You are associating praise with something your dog wants. Eventually your furry friend will come to crave your praise and this will be his reward. Another thing to keep in mind while training is that your dog feeds off of your energy level. If you say, "good dog" in a monotone voice your dog won't read a lot of energy in your voice and body language and might not understand that what he did was appreciated. Instead say, "Good Dog!" and have a lot of excitement, inflection, and energy in your voice. Your pet will feed off this energy and training sessions will be kept fun and upbeat. Don't be embarrassed to make a big deal when your dog finally sits, even if you are in a public place. This is a big moment! It is important that he knows he has just done something amazing. He will know that from the verbal praise and enthusiasm you exude.

Another thing to keep in mind is to not reward partial compliance. Make sure your pet fully complies with the command before rewarding him. If your dog is only half sitting, don't teach him that is the correct position for him to be in by giving him a treat. Make sure he follows the command to completion before reward. We don't want to confuse our pupil as to what the command really means.

Likewise during our training, we want to be mindful of overusing the word "no". We want these training lessons to be upbeat and positive. The golden rule is: "Keep it fun". "No" should be reserved for when your pet is doing something wrong. We don't want to use "no" if he just doesn't understand the meaning of a command yet.

Another one of the key tips to training is to maintain a level of self-assurance and success. If your furry friend never succeeds he will get bored and lose interest. Don't practice a command if you don't think your dog will pay attention or respond. Why set yourselves both up for failure? Failure to respond to a command will teach your dog that it is OK to ignore you. Always end your lesson on a good note. If you see your pet is distracted and bored, finish with an easy command that he knows. When he succeeds, make a big fuss over his achievement and end your lesson.

Finally, keep in mind every dog learns at his own pace. Don't get frustrated if others in your canine obedience class seem to moving at a faster rate. We have trained many dogs and some are just much more in tuned to training lessons. Patterdale terriers are extremely intelligent, but that doesn't necessarily mean they are the easiest type of dog to train. They may appear to have attention deficit disorders, but often it's just that they have their own agenda. Always be calm and consistent and every dog will learn.

This chapter will outline some of the most useful commands for your Pat to know. Once your friend knows these basic commands, you can continue his education with other tutorials. Remember to practice in short intervals to keep it interesting. Don't let him get bored. Keep in mind puppies usually have particularly short attention spans, and if you have a puppy keep lessons very short. It's always better to quit the lesson with your dog wanting more.

HOUSETRAINING

Teaching your dog where it is appropriate to eliminate is undoubtedly the most important training tutorial. This is a lesson we want to begin on the first day of our new friend's arrival. With patience and consistent feedback your new pet will soon let you know on his own when he needs to relieve himself.

One of the keys to effective housetraining is setting your dog up for success and not failure. How will we do this? We will take advantage of our dog's natural instincts to teach him appropriate behavior. For example, most dogs feel the need to eliminate after they wake from a nap or after they eat. When your new friend wakes up or finishes a meal take him outside to where he is expected to relieve himself and wait until he does. When your terrier goes to the bathroom where he is supposed to - praise him lavishly.

Another elimination tendency we can exploit during housetraining is marking. You may notice, before your dog uses the restroom, he sniffs the ground. Dogs have the instinctive habit to pee over other urine smells to mark their territory. As you begin housetraining, bring your four-legged friend to the same spot each time. Here he will smell his own urine and it should trigger him to use the bathroom in this place. It is your dog's natural tendency to re-mark territory; that means it is absolutely essential that you clean up elimination errors properly. If your Patterdale does make an error and pees on your oriental rug, you must remove his urine smell from it or he will likely do it again. To properly clean an area remove all the waste material by soaking it up with paper towels. Then apply an appropriate pet enzymatic cleaner (for example: Nature's Miracle). If you are out of enzymatic cleaner you can use white vinegar to remove pet odor.

A third innate behavior you can leverage for housetraining is your pet's desire to keep his bed clean. This is why crate training is so effective. The rule is simple: when you can't keep an eye on your new Patterdale and he is indoors, he should be in his crate. The size of the crate should be just big enough for him to comfortably sleep. As we mentioned in the puppy chapter, if you purchased a bigger crate for your Patterdale puppy to grow into, divide off part of his crate. You don't want your new friend to have a space to snooze and a separate area of his crate to eliminate in. If he does, you're setting him up for failure. Make sure the area inside his crate is just big enough for him to restfully sleep in.

Now you're setting your untrained Patterdale up for success. You're making sure he's taken outside frequently and particularly when he wakes from naps and after he eats. You're making sure to keep returning him to the same spot for consistency and appropriately cleaning soiled areas indoors. You're keeping him in his crate when you can't watch him. So what do you do when your dog makes a mistake? If you're following the housetraining guidelines you're not giving your dog the chance to make many mistakes. If he does you need to use it as a learning opportunity.

If you catch your Patterdale in the act of relieving himself in the wrong place, you should utter a stern "No" or "Bad" followed by taking him to the right place and waiting until he finishes his business. The severity of your voice should be such that he knows he did something wrong but not enough to scare him. When he goes in the correct place let him know by praising him. What shouldn't you do? Don't rub your dog's nose in his waste and don't hit him even when mistakes are made. This would just teach your dog to develop fear issues.

Eventually, you will know what time during the day your dog needs to go and the two of you will have a routine. Some dogs will eventually let you know that they need to go outside by sitting in front of the door (actually your Patterdale is much more likely to jump repeatedly on the door to indicate his desire). The point is to get into a routine that works for you and your furry friend.

COME/RECALL

It is vital that your Patterdale Terrier knows and respects the "come" command. This is the command that very credibly will save his life. Patterdales are inherently curious and brave with a strong prey drive. These traits can easily propel your dog into traffic chasing a squirrel. He needs to know what "come" means and he needs to immediately respond to that command above all distractions.

There are a couple steps to getting your dog to respond to the "come" command without exception. The first is to get him to understand what the command means. This is a simple, enjoyable step. While there are no distractions, hold a treat or your pet's favorite toy. Call his name followed by "come", in a lively up-beat voice. When he comes, give him a treat or his toy along with excited praise. Repeat this exercise often, keeping with the no distractions rule. You can even make practice of this lesson a fun game with your family. Have two or more family members spread around a room. One at a time, each person will call your dog to come with a treat in hand. When your dog complies, that person can give him a treat and lavish praise. After one minute have the next person call him. As a tip remember to stop this game before your Patterdale gets bored (or full if you're using treats).

Once your dog understands the command it is time to begin adding distance and distractions. Like all training exercises set your dog up for success and not failure. Don't jump into calling your dog when there is a cat on the other side of the window. There's no way he is going to comply. If you do, you're just teaching him it's OK to ignore you. Take the next baby step by calling him from another room and then add distractions. As you add progressively more difficult diversions, you may come to a point where he chooses not to follow your command. At this point we need to begin to employ our first training aid: the long line.

Attach the long line to your dog's collar then call your dog to come with a strong distraction. We he doesn't immediately comply use the long line to calmly direct him toward you. When utilizing the long line the key is to guide your dog not force him. You don't want to get into a tug of war with your pet. When he gets to you praise him and give him a treat. With consistent training you should have a reliable recall with your Patterdale.

There may be occasions where you may need to employ another tool to train recall. This tool is really only necessary if you have a particularly headstrong Patterdale. We have a very willful alpha male that required us to employ an electronic collar. Our Patterdale is a fervent digger and a Houdini-like escape artist. Guests would occasionally not fully shut the kitchen door and he would simply push open the door and take off. This was a dangerous situation as there is a road that runs right in front of our house.

He is a smart little guy. He knows when he's off leash and would choose to ignore us as he explored the neighborhood (until we started the car, that always got him to come running). Understanding his abilities and fortitude, we had to employ an electronic collar to reinforce recall training. Now the key to using an e-collar is to not abuse it or produce a fearful dog. It should simply be an extension of long lead training. Consult your electronic collar manual for proper fit. Don't put it on your Patterdale right before a training session or he will soon learn to hate it. Put on in the morning before you first let him out. It will become part of his routine. He gets a collar and gets to run out-side or go for a walk, now he has positive associations with it being put on.

Later in the day during recall training, call your dog with the "come" command while holding down the continuous stimulus delivery button on your receiver. You will start with the lowest electronic collar setting, preferably just vibrate. When your dog comes to you let go of the button. You are teaching your pet that he should always come to you when called or he will experience discomfort. As distraction level increases, while chasing a cat for instance, you may need to increase the stimulus level. Only do this if he isn't responding to recall at the lowest level. Your goal is to receive an immediate response each time regardless of what is going on around him. The come command can be particularly challenging for Patterdales especially if they are on the chase for prey. Of course always reward you dog for complying with the recall command even during e-collar training.

We only utilize e-collar training for recall lessons, as it is so very critical that he obey this command. Another note on electronic use: it is very easy to produce improper negative associations with its use and you need to be very careful if you employ it. For example, our Patterdale loves to run around with sticks and play keep away from the other dogs in the backyard. So even though he is distracted, we don't practice e-collar recall sessions during these times. The reason is simple: he's playing with a stick and his friends and having fun. He's not in a position where he could harm himself. By utilizing the electronic collar at this time there is a potential that we may send him a message that playing with sticks produces a negative result. We don't want to risk sending that message.

One last thing to mention about use of the "come" command: Never, ever call your dog to come to you and then discipline him. You would in effect be teaching him that coming to you can have negative consequences. This would be extremely detrimental to his education.

WATCH

Watch is an easy command for your dog to learn and a critical building block for many more complicated commands that will require your Patterdale's attention on you. It also helps them learn their name and enforces positive behavior and focus.

To teach "watch", let your dog see a treat and then move it to your nose. When his gaze meets yours say, "good (insert dog's name here), watch" and give him a treat and praise. Remember to smile! Wait until he stops paying attention to you and then repeat. We want to gradually increase the time he holds his attention to your face. At first give him the treat immediately when he looks at you, and then add a second or two at a time before the reward. Don't worry if the dog looks away, just skip the reward and try again.

Once you are confident with your dog's watch ability you can test his strength by creating distractions. Have a family member or friend create a distraction. For the ultimate test of his ability you can take him to a public place where there is a lot of noise such as a park. The "watch" command is a very effective tool to teach your dog to pay attention to you. It is best to teach this command in the early stages of his education, as it is a building block for other more complex commands.

SIT

The "sit" command is a fairly easy instruction for your dog to learn. You can either stand in front of your dog or put your dog in heel position (on your left side with the dogs' right shoulder even with your left leg). In a positive tone, say your dog's name followed by "sit". While the dog is still standing, place the treat close to his nose. Slowly move the treat up and behind the dogs head to bring the dogs head back. Your dog should naturally sit. If he does not sit, you can place your hand gently on his backside and push him downward. As you are moving him down slowly say: "sit".

As soon as the dog sits, give him a treat and a large amount of praise. If the dog does not sit, please don't repeat the "sit" command over and over. If you continue to repeat "sit" you will prolong his understanding of this command. You should train your dog so that he knows that after the first command he needs to sit. In this way, he will learn to pay attention to things you say.

Over time you will want to add more time to how long you're your dog sits before you give him his treat. Add a second or two at each training session until he can sit for 10 seconds before being rewarded. You will want to eventually wean the dog from treats. Work with your dog until you are able to give them a treat about a tenth of the time. Continue to always verbally praise your dog, even if there is no treat. Remember, the best reward is praise and attention from you.

Figure 46: The "sit" command is the basis for many other training commands. "Magoo" and "Jess", photograph used with permission by Mel Mew.

DOWN

Once you are comfortable with the "sit" command, you can move to the "down" command. The "down" command is a submissive and vulnerable position for your terrier to be in. It will most likely not be an easy command for your dog to learn, as it is not a natural position for him to be in. The "down" command can be an important exercise for a stubborn dog so he can come to understand your leadership status in the pack.

To practice the "down" command, start with your dog in the "sit" position. Say your dog's name followed by "down" while you move a treat downward in front of him towards the floor. This will encourage your pet to lower his head and neck. As soon as his belly hits the floor praise him with a "good down!" and give him a treat. Repeating the word "down" as he completes the act will reinforce the behavior.

Figure 47: "Voodoo", practicing the "down" command.
Photograph taken May 2010 in Atlanta, GA, USA.

If your dog is struggling with getting his rear on the ground you can apply some gentle pressure to help him along. As he is moving downward with the front of his body, gently press his back and as he lowers to the ground repeat the command "down" as he meets the floor. If he resists and is not moving to the floor, don't push him too hard. Try moving the treat downward and underneath his chest to encourage them to go "down".

As your dog becomes more comfortable with the command, you will want to slowly wean off treats. Over time just give a treat every third time he completes the down. Regardless, always make sure that the treat is only given if he goes "down" with no help or force.

STAY

Training your dog to stay can also be a challenging command, particularly if he is used to following you around. Keep it simple and build on your Pat's successes. "Stay" can be a useful command if you have guests over or if you have a dog that likes to bolt out of the front door. Some owners use the command when stopping to cross a street to make sure that the dog waits.

Begin practice of the "stay" command when your Patterdale is a little more calm than normal; try working on it after they have had some exercise or a walk. Start by placing the dog in a position that you would like for them to stay in, whether that be a "sit" or "down" position. Stand directly in front of your dog and after a few seconds reward with a treat. Add a second or two on each time you practice. If the dog gets up at any point during the stay, do not scold him. Quickly and firmly place him back in his position.

As a next step, associate the word "stay" with a hand motion and the behavior. Command your dog to "stay" while placing your hand about a foot in front of his face. Take a step back by one foot. Start doing this for 2 to 3 seconds and build up to 10-second stays, all the while keeping it fun. Return back to the dog and offer him a treat and much praise, enforcing the positive behavior with a "Good stay!" Gradually increase the distance between you and your dog during the practice "stay". Eventually you should be able to go into another room.

Some dogs will have difficulty with the "stay" command because they lose concentration or become bored. Remember to start with short time intervals and build up to longer ones. Never keep a dog in a long extended "stay" that lasts for more than a few minutes. You want to let your dog know that when you say: "stay" you will be returning shortly. Long "stays" or saying: "stay" and then leaving the house for 15 minutes will cause the dog to be confused about what the command means.

Practice with the "stay" command should work to include distractions. If you find issues with distractions you can employ the long lead as a tool. Attach the long lead to your pet and then have it go around something stable behind him like a table leg or tree. Put him in the stay position and take steps backward. By holding the lead you can prevent him from moving toward you. If he stands up put him back in the "sit" and repeat, "stay" as you move away. Remember to always come back and reward your dog after a successful "stay". Remember your Patterdale has boundless energy and sitting still is probably not his strongest suit. Calm demeanor and patience are the key behavior elements here.

AROUND

"Around" is a command we like to use because it puts our furry friend in a great position for lessons like "walk" and "heel" or games like Frisbee and fetch. It is normally an extremely simple lesson for our brilliant Patterdales. Have your dog sit or stand facing you. With a treat in your right hand say "around" and lead your dog around both of your legs going in from the right and emerging on your left side. Always go in the same direction when repeating this exercise. This puts your dog in a perfect position to start a walk on the left side of you or chase a Frisbee that you have thrown.

WALK

There will come a time when you will want to take your dog for a walk. Depending on how you have prepared, this can be a fun and easy task or a difficult and physically exhausting one. Teaching your dog to walk by your side without pulling can be challenging for a Patterdale Terrier who is always picking up new scents and tracking down prey. A little practice is all you will need, however, to incorporate pleasurable dog walks in to your daily routine.

Always start your dog walking on your left. Say, "let's walk!" and move forward starting with your left leg. Keep the leash loose, if possible. If your dog is walking at your left side and not pulling encourage them with a "good walk!" In the beginning, always continue to praise your dog if they are walking correctly. If he is pulling forward or to the side, give him a quick pop of the leash directing him back toward your left side. Never yell at or discourage the dog. You want him to want to be by you, and negative reinforcement will only push him away.

Try taking walks around your neighborhood using the "let's walk" command. Do not let the dog pull. Many dogs will want to pull you. In that case just turn around and start heading the other way or stop walking and give him a pop on the lead. Wait until the lead gets slack and then begin again. If the dog pulls excessively, you may want to try a "pinch" collar. It is not as cruel as it sounds. A pinch collar gently pinches your dog's neck, preventing him from pulling. If he is not pulling, there is no pinch. A veterinarian invented the pinch collar as a safe alternative to choke chains. Pinch collars are best for smaller dogs like Patterdale Terriers because choke collars can damage a small dog's trachea. Pinch collars should only be used during the training stages. If you have never used a pinch collar, make sure you consult someone who has, like a dog trainer, to insure proper use.

HEEL

Once you have your dog walking with you and he understands the "watch" command, you can introduce "heel" to him. The "heel" command requires motion coupled with attention. Heel is a high-level focused "watch" in motion. It can help you in dangerous situations where you need your dog to walk by your side or when they are off leash.

To practice heel, stand in front of your dog with a treat. Keep the treat at waist level. With the leash in your left hand and the treat in your right say, "let's walk". Take a step backward and then turn around facing the same direction as your dog saying "heel".

It is this motion of alignment with your dog that is known as the "heel position". His ears should be about even with your thigh. At the point where you turn your body around, you will want to place the treat several inches away from the dogs' nose and keep it here while you are making the turn. Move forward walking in a straight line. Take several steps forward and then reward the dog with a treat.

The first few times you practice this you will want to only walk forward in the "heel" position for a few steps. Add a step here and there throughout your training up to about a dozen steps. "Heel" is not to be used on your everyday walks, as it is meant to teach your dog to move with you momentarily, while paying attention. It should be used in situations where your dog becomes free of his leash in public or if there is a dangerous situation where you need him to stay close and pay attention.

Once you are comfortable getting your dog to "walk" and "heel", you can start from the heel position. Get your dog's attention by using the "watch" command. Say "heel" and take a short step ahead. If your dog remains in "heel" position, reward him with a treat and praise. Over time you will want to add a step, and then another step, and so on. You may find it helpful to talk to your dog while he is walking in "heel" position, engaging his attention. The end goal is for your dog's attention to be on your face while he is walking in the "heel" position.

STAND

Teaching your dog to "stand" can be a useful tool if you are planning on introducing your dog to the conformation or show ring. In the show ring, your dog will be required to stand while he is inspected. Standing is a predecessor to "stacking" which is an essential show procedure.

To practice standing, have your dog sit next to you on your left side. Say, "stand" while pulling his leash with your right hand and moving your left foot forward. As soon as he stands up reward him with a treat and a "Good stand!"

Figure 48: "Sahara" is poised in good "stand" position.
Photo taken in September, 2014 in Atlanta, GA, USA.

If you are training your dog to "stand" for competitions, you should also have your friends and family touch the dog while in a stand position so he can get comfortable with it. He will need to be used to having his teeth and reproductive organs touched. If the judge sees that your dog can stand while they check your dog over they will see that you have a well-behaved dog.

Have your friends and family start with the dogs face and have the dog sniff their hand so that he feels more comfortable with who is touching them. Once they have touched the face have them rub their hands down the dog's sides, down each leg, down the tail and then back up to the face. All of this will be done while the dog is in a "stand" position. If your dog sits, correct him back to "stand" position.

Another way to get your dog to stand is from a lying down position. Gently slide your hand under his stomach until he begins to stand. As soon as he begins to stand slowly say, "stand" and reward him. You can also try this technique from a sit position. Face your dog, holding a favorite toy or treat. As you step back your dog will probably stand up to reach the treat or toy. When he does, praise and reward him with the treat. Whether lying or sitting you may need to keep your hand under your dog's belly until he is steady and standing for a couple of seconds.

CONCLUSION

Training is an adventure with many ups and downs. We hope that as you embark on your training journey, you encounter many more rewarding moments than trying ones. Just remember to practice training when both you and your dog are in the right frame of mind to do so. If your dog hasn't had much exercise that day, try taking him on a walk to release some of his energy before jumping right into training. Likewise, if you have had a long day and are tired, you may want to skip training that day as you will want to be refreshed and filled with patience before teaching and bonding with your dog.

"Owning a working terrier without allowing it to work is like owning a vintage bottle of wine so you can read the label."

Patrick Burns (a.k.a. "The Terrierman")

Figure 49: "Nogger", taken in the forest of Wiblengen in Ulm, Germany. Photograph used with permission by Ralph Rückert.

[10]

Game On!

THERE ISN'T A DAY that goes by that we aren't held in awe over Voodoo the Patterdale Terrier's latest amusement. Now it would be brilliant if these were enjoyable games of fetch with his owners in the backyard, but that wouldn't be his style. Voodoo is a likeable bully, a tormentor by nature. If we are playing fetch with one of our other dogs, Voodoo will quickly snatch the ball and change the game into one of keep away. Voodoo also has a strange fascination with inanimate objects he feels are not appropriately respecting his position in the household. He frequently digs up antique treasures in the backyard and then proceeds to bark at them, prance around the yard with them, and then shred them to bits. He has found old soccer balls, bottles, even a large bone of questionable origin. He really isn't selective at all. If a 15-pound branch has the nerve to fall in his lawn, his reaction is quite the same - furious barking before carrying it off into the depths of the backyard for its decapitation and amputation. We can no longer have plastic pots full of flowers in on the back deck, as he will quickly run off with those and shred them and their rooted contents to fragments. His latest game is even more ingenious. He has taken to wrestling with the garden hose and chewing off four-foot sections at a time. He then runs up and down the chain-link fence separating our yard from the neighbors, his new prize rattling against the fence, much like a prison warden to awaken inmates. He does this intentionally to infuriate the dogs next door and entice them to play tug of war with him through the fencing with the hose. If only we had an ounce of his energy...

ENERGY TO BURN

To say that the Patterdale Terrier is energetic would be a flagrant understatement. Your Pat's energy is boundless and will encircle yours many times over. Even after regular exercise with your Patterdale, you will find those occasions when you come home and your furry friend still insists on running rings around the living room. Terriers and Patterdales in particular love to run, chase, and play – providing the opportunity for many different activities for you both to engage in. Your Patterdale Terrier is highly intelligent and brimming with drive. It would be a crime not to provide opportunities for him to take part in as many activities as possible. Keep in mind, if you don't find an outlet for his energy he will find one on his own and chances are you won't like his choice. Whether you attend terrier trials or enjoy activities around the house, there are plenty of options that are fun for everyone involved. It just depends on where your interests lie and what your energy level is. Is your energy more of a 3 or an 8 on a 10 scale? Undoubtedly, your Patterdale's energy level will be turned up to eleven!

If you have the chance to take part in terrier trials they can be a great deal of fun for you and your Patterdale. They are a wonderful way to meet and mingle with other dog lovers and their canine companions. If you are thinking about entering competitions, you may want to learn how to train and prepare. The best way to do this is to find a local terrier group that meets consistently to practice and have fun. If you can't find a local Patterdale Terrier club, see if you can find and/or join a Jack Russell Terrier club to meet up with. The two types of dogs were both bred for similar hunting purposes and often the Jack Russell Terrier clubs will have members with other terrier breeds like Patterdales.

In the United States, the Jack Russell Terrier Club of America (JRTCA) is a very large consortium that holds many terrier activities. At these events there will often be classes open to all terrier breeds or specific classes for "colored terriers". These classes are put in place for breeds like Patterdales, Lakelands, Borders, and other terrier types at JRTCA competitions.

The Patterdale Terrier was bred to track and pursue fox, and his personality and intellect are testament to this. His body is of compact and balanced proportion, designed with a small chest. The Patterdale Terrier's body is very flexible, allowing him to move around through small spaces underground. This conformation allows the Patterdale to chase his quarry down narrow tunnels. The fox is a good model for the size of the Patterdale: where the fox can maneuver, so must the Patterdale. Although originally bred for fox hunting, the Patterdale is a versatile working terrier for a variety of different quarry. As Patterdales are working terriers, most sporting competitions for his type are geared towards mimicking their natural hunting instincts.

Go-To-Ground

A working terrier is defined as any small dog that pursues their quarry, or hunted animal, into the ground. As fox hunting became popular in Britain in the 18th and 19th centuries, canines such as the Patterdale Terrier were bred to hunt red fox as well as Eurasian badger. These quarry were hunted in their underground burrows. This later became known as "terrier work" or "going to ground". Most terrier trials will host Go-To-Ground (GTG) competitions. This is an exciting contest where you can watch your Patterdale ignite his innate primal DNA to pursue quarry.

Figure 50: "Voodoo", at his first go-to-ground event as a puppy.
Photograph taken at the Terrier Olympics in June, 2010 in Gray, TN, USA.

Go-To-Ground events are designed to test your dog's intrinsic ability to work underground. In competitions, your pet will be released two feet from the entrance of a man-made tunnel. Your Patterdale is expected to move through the tunnel as fast as he can until he reaches the end. At the end of the tunnel there is a grate, and on the other side of that grate is a rat in a cage. Your Patterdale will then be expected to "work" his quarry for a set amount of time based on the class he is in. "Working" can mean barking, whining, digging, and/or scratching. These competitions are timed with the fastest dogs recognized and awarded, usually as "Champion" and "Reserve Champion".

Will a good Go-to-Ground dog make a good hunting terrier? It is certainly not necessarily true, but it is the closest some Patterdales ever get to any type of work below the earth. Even though GTG is really more or less a game for the Patterdales, it is a good training step towards the day your Patterdale may do real earthwork. It simulates their natural instinct to do what they were bred for, and is undoubtedly a fun activity for them.

Training a Patterdale puppy to play in tunnels can be rewarding and fun to watch. For puppies that are still small, we suggest picking up a ten-foot section of 6-inch diameter PVC pipe you'll find at most hardware stores. With a simple hacksaw you can cut that pipe into three pieces. Then attach all three pieces to a Y-connector you can find at the same hardware store. Now you have a beginner tunnel gym for your puppy. The Y-connector will ensure the tunnel stays stable and doesn't roll when your puppy enters it. The PVC will stand up well to the elements, which makes this a great toy for play indoors or outside.

The two keys to this training are to make it fun and avoid any fearful associations. The Y-connector is helping us keep the toy stable, which avoids potential fearful associations. Let your puppy explore this tunnel on his own; just watch for a few minutes. Does he immediately crawl inside? Great, you may have a natural. Is he curious of the tunnel? Does he sniff around the entryways and peek his head in? We can work with that. Take a treat and put it a few inches inside the entry and then another a foot inside the entry. Gradually put the treats deeper and deeper into the tunnel. Your furry friend will soon get the idea that tunnels are a good thing and will be running through them in no time. Now remember: we don't want fearful associations, so avoid banging or tapping on the tunnel with your puppy inside. When your pup first crawls and exits from another side make a big fuss over him to let him know how special he is. We often send wind-up toy hamsters through the tunnels for our puppies to chase and pull out. You can also throw in your pet's favorite toy. Make the tunnel a fun game to play between the two of you. On a side note, we advise against introducing live animals to your puppy training at this stage. Just keep it a light and fun game. We're trying to focus on making tunnels a great game at this point.

As your dog approaches six months of age old and gets larger, or if you start training with an older dog, you may want to start building a more official GTG tunnel. For a great tutorial on building a tunnel see the Early Training section of Patrick Burns book, *American Working Terriers* (Burns, 2005). This book has great step-by-step instructions for building your first 6-foot tunnel out of ¾ inch plywood sheets. There are also detailed guidelines for building long tunnels. Alternatively, plans are available online from the AKC Earthdog site.

Using quarry may or may not be your next step in tunnel training. How do you know if your dog is ready? According to the Terrierman, "while getting a dog to run a tunnel is largely a learned behavior, a dog's reaction to quarry is largely instinctive and age-dependent." If you are serious about training and have the desire and ability to keep a rat it is definitely the best way to train your Patterdale for upcoming GTG trials. For more information, refer to the American Working Terriers book. Patrick's book contains a wealth of information on training your dog at home with quarry.

To get a little better understanding of GTG events, the interior dimensions of the tunnels are 9" wide by 9" of height. For novice events, a ten-foot tunnel with one bend is used. For open and certificate classes a thirty-foot tunnel with two bends is used. In all cases a rat (the quarry) is held in a cage at the end of the tunnel. A Go-To-Ground trial will have various officials including a judge, a paddock steward, and a den steward. The sanctioned judge will evaluate the terrier on his ability to work the quarry. He will time the dog through the tunnel. The paddock steward assembles exhibitors, collects GTG sheets, and keeps the spectators away from the tunnels. The den steward will check the paperwork and record judges' comments.

Figure 51: Patterdales instinctively hunt.
"Finta", photograph used with permission by
Zuzana Hodová (Kennel Srdcové eso).

When it is your turn, your terrier is to be placed two feet in front of the tunnel. All four of your dog's feet must be touching the ground. The GTG judge will ask you to release your terrier when you are ready. Your Patterdale will be expected to move through the tunnel as fast as he can. At the end of the tunnel will be a grate over the opening to keep the terrier from harming the quarry.

A GTG judge times the terrier from the moment it is released until it begins to "work" the quarry. Depending upon the class entered the terrier must mark the quarry for a set period of time (typically thirty seconds to a minute). If the terrier successfully works the quarry, the time is recorded. If the dog is unsuccessful in working the quarry, the dog is disqualified.

The judge will let you know when it is time to release your dog. After a dog is released, the handler is to remain near the entrance hole. Once the dog has entered, the handler may not block the entrance hole by standing front of in it or in any other manner. Training commands and encouragement are allowed. The judge will signal to the exhibitor to pick up the dog at the completion of his work. Handlers are not allowed to tap on the tunnel or retrieve their dog until the judge indicates it is time to do so. Any violation of this rule will result in disqualification of the terrier from the class.

The Go-To-Ground competition is normally comprised of three class divisions: Novice, Open and Championship. In the Novice and Open class divisions the requirements are the same: to score a 100% by reaching the quarry in less than one minute and working the quarry for 30 seconds. The dog may leave the earth, or tunnel, and re-enter in Novice and Open classes. The Novice class is separated into Pre-Novice, Novice Puppy and Novice Adult subclasses. The Novice classes are open to dogs that have not scored 100% at a previous trial.

The Pre-Novice Puppy is open to pups 4 to 6 months of age. They are allowed one minute to reach the quarry and they must mark the quarry for 15 seconds. They are allowed to leave the earth and re-enter. The Novice Puppy is open to pups 6 to 12 months of age. They are allowed 1 minute to reach the quarry and must work the quarry for 30 seconds. They are allowed to leave and re-enter the earth. If the dog earns a score of 100% they may be allowed to enter the Open class.

The Novice Adult is open to dogs one year of age or older. They are allowed 1 minute to reach the quarry and must work the quarry for 30 seconds. They are allowed to leave and re-enter the earth. Participants are allowed to move into the Open class upon successfully completing a novice test.

The Open class is also split into Puppy and Adult subclasses. The Open classes are open to dogs that have scored 100% in a Novice Go-To-Ground class at the current trial or a previous trial. In both classes dogs are allowed 30 seconds to reach the quarry and must work the quarry for one minute. They are allowed to leave the earth once.

The Open Puppy Class is open to dogs 6-12 months of age. (The Open Puppy Class is open to pups that have already successfully completed the Novice Puppy Class.) Puppies are allowed to leave the earth once. Puppies that finish this class may move on to the Puppy Championship GTG class. The Open Adult Class is for dogs one year or older and follows the same guidelines as the Open Puppy Class.

The Championship Classes are split into Puppy and Adult categories and are accessible to dogs that earn 100% to Open GTG (30 foot tunnel). Dogs are allowed thirty seconds to reach the quarry and must work for one minute. In the championship classes, dogs are at no time allowed to leave the earth.

Finally, a Veteran Championship is open to any adult dog 6 years of age or older, who holds a Trial Certificate. Here, 30 seconds are allowed to reach the quarry and the dog must work the quarry for one minute. Dogs are not allowed to leave the earth.

Super Earth

Now let's move on to the next level of fun. Super Earth is like Go-To-Ground on steroids! Super Earth events are tricky Go-To-Ground courses, which consist of false entrances, water hazards and other puzzles and barriers your terrier must overcome to reach the quarry at the end. Each dog is allowed 30 seconds per 30 foot of tunnel to reach the quarry and must work the prey for one minute. This event is a wonderful challenge for your furry companion. Super Earth setups are so variable from event to event, each with different obstacles. It's a real treat to see how your Pat will think, learn, and adapt to realize his final goal.

Barn and Brush Hunt

These competitions focus on your Patterdale's fantastic nose and his ability to use it to sniff out prey. In Barn Hunt, a rat in a cage is hidden in a simulated barn environment (usually utilizing hay bales). Your dog is released at a designated area and timed to the point when he finds the rat. The dog with the fastest time is recognized as the winner. Brush hunt is very similar, except a rat is hidden in a fenced-off forested area.

Figure 52: "Tara" doing Barn Hunt, March 2014.
Photograph used with permission by Cathy Thomas.

Training your Pat to use his nose is fun and easy. The simplest way may be to start in your house. While your dog is out of the room, take a treat and put it in the middle of the floor. Bring your dog into the room and in and upbeat voice say, "Find the treat". Lavish him with praise when he succeeds. Every time you practice this game make finding the treat harder, putting it behind doors and under furniture. These exercises will help him tune his nose and are great fun!

Next, graduate to hiding treats outside. Ultimately you want to provide opportunities where he has the opportunity to practice finding a real rat in a cage hidden outdoors. Once again, local terrier clubs are great options for this type of practice. When training to find a rat you may want to change the phrase to "Find the Rat!" so he learns to differentiate what he is expected to do with his amazing nose.

Figure 53: Patterdales love to participate in Brush Hunt.
If they don't normally get a chance to hunt, this is a good substitute.
Photograph taken in February, 2011 at
the Gold Coast Terrier Network trial in Bronson, FL, USA.

TRAIL & LOCATE

Trail & locate terrier contests are another great outlet for your Patterdale to apply that remarkable nose of his. In this event, a rat in a cage is hidden in an outdoor area. A scent trail is created leading to the rat. This scent trail is usually created using fox urine. Scoring is based on the time to mark the quarry as well as accuracy for following the scent trail. The intent of this exercise is to simulate, as closely as possible, a natural hunting environment.

Fox urine can be purchased online for training at home. When practicing at home, make a scent trail that ends in a rat, or a treat if you don't have access to a live rat. Release your Patterdale at the start of the scent trail and say, "Find the Rat!" Once again lavish him with praise when he reaches his quarry (or treat).

LURE COURSING

Lure Coursing is a fast-paced chase sport. This is generally just about every dog's favorite event at a terrier competition. Most dogs take to the lure right away and it generally requires very little in the way of training. In lure coursing, dogs run after a mechanically operated lure (usually a white plastic bag) that is attached to a line that is controlled by a machine and a lure operator. The lure operator determines the lure speed, keeping it just in front of the dog's view as to not lose his interest. It follows a dog's natural prey behavior, allowing him to run free and fast, and is great fun for him. It is also entertaining for us humans to watch.

Figure 54: "Voodoo" practicing lure coursing at the
Cartersville Saddle Club in September 2010 in Cartersville, GA, USA.

A typical lure course is between 600 and 1000 yards (548 to 914 meters) long. Some courses incorporate obstacles or jumps; others are simply set in a large circle. The track can be fenced or open. In competitions, dogs are given two turns around the course. The fastest time is recorded and winners are rewarded ribbons or prizes.

Figure 55: "Voodoo" taking his turn at lure coursing.
Photograph taken in February 2011 at
the Gold Coast Terrier Network's trial in Bronson, FL.

At the starting line, dogs are straining to run and highly motivated by the sight of the lure. Your running dog is usually so intensely focused on chasing the lure that there is little fear of him running off course or leaving the field. At the end of the run the lure returns to the starting line with your dog in hot pursuit. It is an intense workout for him, so make sure to provide ample water at the end of his run. You may want to dip your dog in a water bath after each run to cool him down, especially on hot summer days.

TERRIER RACING

There is one sport that brings out human passion surpassing all others at most every terrier event – racing! This is particularly true in the southern United States where racing is king, regardless if that contest is between 3400-pound automobiles or 15-pound dogs. There is something about placing a muzzled terrier into a starting box next to five other canine athletes, seeing that flag come down, and viewing all the dogs leaping out together, chasing a lure towards a finish hole that gets spectators' hearts pumping. Terrier racing is fast-paced, emotional, and extremely fun.

Terrier racing comes in different flavors to add interest and texture to competitions. The big two are flat and hurdle (or steeplechase) racing. Both of these events are held on a straight course with a measured distance of 150 to 225 feet long. Hurdle racing, as the name implies, has the addition of four (or more) evenly spaced hurdles along the track, at least 20 feet apart. These hurdles have a height of 16 inches for adult dogs or 8 inches for puppies.

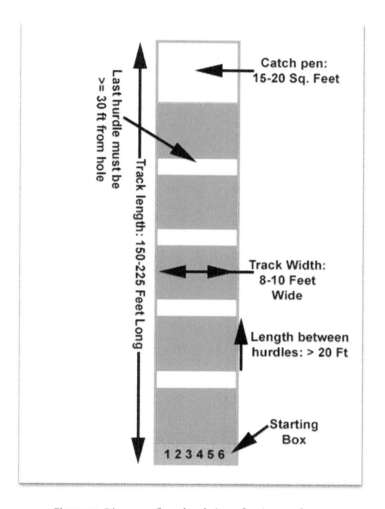

Figure 56: Diagram of overhead view of racing track.

All canine racing contestants are required to wear muzzles for the protection of catchers and other dogs. Competitions employ colorful fabric racing collars for the dogs to assist in the identification of the contenders' order of finish. The racetrack begins with a starting box that can hold six canine competitors. The starting box is at least 15 inches high with the front hatch composed of Plexiglas or strong wire mesh, so the dogs can view the lure. The lure (generally a piece of fur but could also be a simple plastic bag) is attached to a motorized pull that drags it from the starting box all the way through the finish hole at the end of the track and into the catch pen. The finish hole marks the end of the course. It is 15 inches tall by 8 inches wide and was traditionally constructed from straw bales. Today, backstops are usually molded from vinyl-covered foam as it safer for the high-speed canine collisions that inevitably occur as dogs hurdle themselves simultaneously through the small opening.

Figure 57: A starting box for racing, as seen from the dog-loading side.
Photograph taken June 2010 at the Terrier Olympics in Gray, TN, USA.

The official finish line is on the other side of the ending hole (this can lead to some interesting finales as the first terrier to enter the hole isn't always the first to come out!). Once all canine athletes are in the catch pen, six humans (referred to as "catchers") scramble to pick up the pups and return them to their owners.

Introducing your Patterdale to racing is best done through a local terrier club. These clubs will often have the equipment (the starting box, backstop, and motorized pulley) available for practice meet-ups. Don't forget you will need to purchase a muzzle for your dog to wear. Many dogs get very worked up and excited at this event and you wouldn't want any fights to break out. There are two types of muzzles: the basket and the softie muzzle. Basket muzzles are generally favored, as they do seem to allow for easier breathing for your pup. While many Pats instinctively take off chasing the lure others may need some time and numerous practice runs to understand the game.

At home you can begin training by getting your dog used to chasing a fur (or plush animal with the stuffing removed). Begin by teasing your Pat with the lure and playing some tug games with it. Next attach the lure to some string and have your dog chase after it. You can attach the string to a stick (known as a flirt pole) to make the game more challenging. Run the lure over objects to prepare him for jumping over hurdles.

Figure 58: In terrier racing, dogs are released from the starting box and lured to the catch pen by a stuffed plush toy. These terriers are racing at the Gold Coast Terrier Network Trial in February 2012 in Bronson, FL, USA.

Another item to practice at home is positive association with a muzzle. Most all dogs will initially rebel against wearing a muzzle, so expect for your dog to try to pull it off with his paws. Introduce the muzzle slowly to your Patterdale. A good trick is to hold the muzzle in your hand and put a little peanut butter on the inside. Hold it so your furry friend will need to poke his nose in and lick it off. Gradually work up to buckling it on for just a second and then immediately removing it, all while praising your dog fervently. Increase the amount of time before removing the buckle and of course continue to lavish him with praise and maybe even a treat. We are building up the muzzle as a good thing that always comes with praise and treats. Keep this exercise up and in no time his muzzle will be accepted as another tool, like his leash, and associated with positive thoughts.

Figure 59: A Patterdale clears a hurdle during a steeplechase race.
Photograph taken at the Dogwood JRTC Trial
in September 2010 in Cartersville, GA, USA.

Always remember that racing is a very strenuous activity, especially on warm days. Always have water available for your furry friend. Most events will have a pool available for terriers to cool off after a run. Remember to keep the events fun. Don't expect to walk away with a first place ribbon your first time out. Practice will make perfect. Expect on initial runs that your Pat may sit confused in the starting box, stop along the racetrack to tug with his muzzle, or turn around and run back to the start. This happens to everyone! Your Patterdale is smart and will eventually understand what he should do. He just needs to practice. Over time, just seeing the muzzle or the starting box will send your Patterdale into frenzy. Another fun variation of racing is muskrat racing. This event is a biathlon where dogs race down a platform and then jump into a pool to swim the last part of the race.

Figure 60: Patterdales race to the finish and fight to see who can enter the hole first.
Photograph taken at the Patterdale Terrier Festival in March 2011 in Ruskin, FL, USA.

DOCK DIVING

First appearing in 1997 at the Purina Incredible Dog Challenge, dock diving is a sport where dog owners vie to see whose canine can jump the farthest from a dock into a body of water. The dock itself is usually 35 to 40 feet long by 8 feet wide and 2 feet above the water surface. The size of the body of water can vary, as long as the water is at least 4 feet deep. In most cases, a pool is used. The dock itself is covered in rubber or artificial turf for safety.

There are two different techniques that can be used to encourage your dog to jump into the water. One is known as "Place and Send". This involves throwing a toy into the water while holding the dog back. "Place" the dog at the starting point, and then release or "send" the dog to get the toy. This technique works well for dogs that are not trained to stay. The other dock diving technique is known as "chase". In this method, the dog is placed in a stay position on the dock. The owner then walks to the end of the dock, where he calls the dog and throws a toy into the water. The toy is kept just in front of the dogs' nose encouraging the dog to "chase" it. The chase method is more difficult, and is best used with dogs that understand the "stay" command. In both techniques it is helpful if the dog is toy-driven.

At dock diving events, each dog takes two jumps in a round-robin format. The longer of the two jumps is used for scoring. The jump is only official when the toy leaves the owners hand. The dog need not retrieve the toy for the jump to count. Jump distance is in most cases measured from the edge of the dock to where the dogs' tail hits the water. Distance is either measured electronically or by judges. A large ruler is attached to the side of the pool for measurement.

There are various divisions of dock jumping. Depending on the sanctioning organization, teams are ranked on how far they jump. They are rated against teams in their division. The UKC added Dock Jumping as one of its recognized sports in 2005. Patterdales can get UKC titles by competing in dock distance or height jumping. In UKC events, dogs can obtain titles in Ultimate Air or Distance jumping, and Ultimate Vertical. In Ultimate Air, handlers try to get their dogs to fly as far as they can after a toy. This is the most basic form of dock jumping. In Ultimate Vertical a bumper is held 8 feet out over the water. An initial height is established and the dog must knock the bumper down to pass. The bumper is then moved up 2 inches per round. This continues until there is only one dog left. It is similar to high jumping for dogs.

Weight Pulling

Many dogs pull by nature, especially when they are on a lead. If this is the case with your dog, you may want to consider the sport of weight pull to release some of his energy. Weight pull is an activity that traces its roots to using animals to transport cargo (known as freighting). While not in the historical roots of the Patterdale terrier, our little dogs generally excel in this activity because of their high strength to weight ratio and unwavering never-quit attitude.

Where do you find weight pulling events? There are a few organizations that can help you. Across the world there is the Global Pulling Alliance. In North America and Europe, the American Pulling Alliance (APA) holds sanctioned weight pulls. Additionally in North America, the International Weight Pull Association (IWPA) and the United Kennel Club (UKC) hold weight pull events.

While rules may differ slightly depending on the governing body and specific event, the core tenants are simple. Each canine athlete is placed in a harness and encouraged to pull a weighted cart a specified distance within an allotted time. Track surfaces are typically made of artificial turf, dirt, carpet, grass, or snow. Dogs are separated into classes by their weight, and ranking is done by how much weight your pet can successfully pull in proportion to his body weight.

If you are interested in trying your dog in weight pulling you should observe an event to see how it works. Weight pulling competitions are often held in conjunction with other working dog events (not specifically terrier trials). If you decide that it is something that you would like to try, you will first need to get a freight harness for your dog. This harness needs to be specifically sized for your pet, to spread the weight evenly and prevent injury to your furry friend.

You will want your Patterdale to understand the "stay" command. For more information on this command, please see our training chapter. Once you place your dog in the harness you will command them to "stay" as you head over to the finish line. At this point you enthusiastically call your dog to "come". To practice weight pulling you will want to get a correctly sized harness and begin conditioning your dog to pulling items. Some ideas are old tires or a child's wagon. Always give lots of praise and encouragement and don't add too much weight too quickly. We want to celebrate his successes and gradually increase weight. Keep training sessions short to avoid hurting your pet or losing his interest.

CANINE GOOD CITIZEN

The Canine Good Citizen (CGC) is a program sponsored by the American Kennel Club (AKC). The AKC offers a certificate to award dogs that are good ambassadors both at home and in the community. This program is open to all dogs, both pure and mixed breeds. The program promotes good behavior in canines and responsible ownership in humans. The CGC program can be seen as a good basic training opportunity for our Patterdales as it prepares them for other activities such as agility and therapy dog training.

The Canine Good Citizen certificate is awarded when owners sign a Responsible Dog Owners Pledge where they agree to take care of their dogs' health, training, safety, and quality of life. In addition, the dog must pass a 10-step behavioral evaluation that includes:

1. Accepting a friendly stranger
2. Sitting politely for petting
3. Allowing basic grooming procedures
4. Walking on a loose lead
5. Walking through a crowd
6. Sitting and lying down on command and staying in place

7. Coming when called
8. Reacting appropriately to another dog
9. Reacting appropriately to distractions
10. Calmly enduring supervised separation from the owner

All items must be completed to satisfaction for success. Treats and toys are not allowed during testing, and all dogs must be on a leash. If a dog eliminates during testing they will be dismissed. Other items for dismissal include growling, snapping, and biting.

AGILITY

Agility is a wonderful sport that showcases the connection between human and canine. In these competitions, a handler directs his canine companion through a complex obstacle course. Scoring is a composition of both time and accuracy. No food or toys can be used to capture your dog's attention at these events, only your voice and hand motions are allowed.

Patterdales have an amazing body awareness and fearless nature that make them very strong contenders. The flip side of the coin is the strong primal drive of our Pat, that doesn't always make pleasing a human trainer a top priority for him. Since agility isn't necessarily utilizing our pet's instinct, this sport will undoubtedly require a significant amount of training for success. But the wonderful thing about all this time spent training is the bond that it creates between Patterdale and owner. Going through agility schooling acts to deepen the relationship your Pat and you will have together. For instruction it is best to find an agility trainer in your area, often found at establishments that do basic obedience classes.

Agility courses are set up by a judge who determines the layout and the obstacles to be used; because of this, all courses are different. Courses are intentionally designed to be difficult enough so that a dog could not complete them without a handler's direction. This is to ensure each handler plays a part in the competition, assessing the course and how to best direct the dog through it. Handlers are allowed a quick walk through before the competition begins to consider the obstacles and make a plan.

The walk through is critical to the success of the event. An agility course can take many different turns, often using the same obstacle more than once. Many times course maps are made available to the handlers prior to competing. Course maps contain obstacles and are numbered to let the handler know the order of complications.

At a competition, dogs and handlers are given one chance to complete the course successfully. Dogs begin at a starting line and progress as quickly and as accurately as possible through each obstacle. Handlers stay close to the dog, directing them through the obstacles. Scoring is based on the number of faults incurred. Faults include things such as knocking over obstacles or exceeding the time limit on the course. The most common obstacles utilized in agility include:

- Dogwalk – consists of three planks, one raised plank (about 4 feet in the air) connected on both ends by one ascending plank and one descending plank. The planks range anywhere from 9 to 12 feet long and 9 to 12 inches in width. The planks may contain slats and/or a rubberized surface to assist with grip.
- Tire/Hoop Jump – a tire-shaped ring is suspended in a frame. The dog is required to jump through the opening.

Figure 61: "Borgoe", participating in a Tire Jump obstacle.
Photo taken in March 2011 in South Miami, FL, USA.
Photograph used with permission by Anouk Boon.

- A-Frame – consists of two ramps hinged together forming an "A" shape. The highest part is typically between 5 and 6 feet. The ramps are typically 3 feet wide and 8 feet long. The bottoms of the ramps are typically painted a bright color indicating the contact zone where the dog must place one paw on the ascent and descent. The frames may have horizontal slats and/or rubberized surfaces.

- Teeter-Totter – similar to a child's seesaw, the teeter-totter obstacle consists of a plank pivoting on a fulcrum. It is constructed so that one side always returns back down to its starting position. This plank does not have slats, but may have a rubberized surface depending on the organization sanctioning the event.

- Tunnel – consists of a vinyl and wire tube that is typically 2 feet in diameter and anywhere from 10 to 20 feet long. The tunnel is flexible so that it can be positioned for various turns, but in many cases it can also just be straight. Sandbags are typically set in place to keep the tunnel from moving.

- Collapsed Tunnel – also known as closed tunnel, a collapsed tunnel is just that – a fabric tunnel that starts out as an open tunnel and ends in a tube of collapsed fabric. The dog runs into the open end and pushes through the collapsed end.

- Bar Hurdle – a bar is set on a hurdle, the height adjusted based on height of the dog.

Figure 62: "Borgoe", photo taken in December 2012 Valrico, FL, USA.
Photograph used with permission by Anouk Boon.

- Spread Hurdle – instead of one bar, two or three bars are used in either a parallel or ascending fashion. The spread is adjusted based on the height of the dog.
- Long Jump – several platforms are placed together to form a wide area that the dog must jump over. This is also referred to as the "platform jump".
- Pause Table – a 3 foot square platform is elevated based on the dogs' height. The dog is required to jump on the table and sit or assume a down position. The dog must remain on the table for a short period of time.
- Weave Poles – one of the most difficult obstacles to master, the weave poles consist of 5 to 12 poles 3 feet tall and 2 feet apart. The dogs are required to enter with the first pole on the left, weaving through each pole without missing one.

Figure 63: "Borgoe", participating in a weave pole obstacle event.
Photo taken in December 2011 in Palmetto, FL, USA.
Photograph used with permission by Anouk Boon.

- Swing Plank – the dog is required to walk over a plank bridge suspended by 4 chains.

DISC DOG (A.K.A. FRISBEE)

Frisbee is another wonderful team activity to play with your Patterdale. Our terriers are strong, intelligent, and fast working dogs with a tireless "can do" attitude. These are all great qualities for Frisbee dog play and competition. Disc dog is a team sport. The team is made up of you and your dog. This teamwork helps build a wonderful bond between you and your furry companion, much like agility. Also, Frisbee play is outstanding for getting our Pats the exercise they need, and building their stamina.

Frisbee, like agility, is a trained ability making success the result of proper education. If you are considering disc dog for your Pat, an obedience class is a good first step. The next stride is to get your dog to build a relationship with his Frisbee. This can be done effortlessly - use a Frisbee as his food dish (note: this should only be done if you're not free feeding as we only want him to have access to this "special" toy when we're around). Feeding from a Frisbee is a particularly good start with puppies. If you're starting with a puppy make sure to get an appropriately sized Frisbee. Another great thing about using Frisbees as food dishes is that they are easily thrown in the dishwasher for cleaning. A great resource for dog discs at the time of this writing is www.skyhoundz.com (the authors have no affiliation with this site).

So now your Pat is eating from his dog disc, what's next? Let's get him used to chasing it. Put a light lead on your dog and get his Frisbee ready. He should be very interested, after all that's his food dish you have there. Crouch down on the ground with your dog and in a highly animated voice start asking your dog if he wants to play "Frisbee". Tease him with the disc and play a light game of tug with your Pat. Tug only for a second or two, and then tell your dog to "release" or "drop". If your dog doesn't understand this command just put one hand over the top of his muzzle and push his lips against his teeth with your fingers and thumb and say, "drop". This will cause your dog to release the disc and learn what "drop" means. Soon he will release on command. Next, slide the disc across the floor to engage his chase instinct. When he grabs the disc, pull him towards you with the lead, enthusiastically calling him "a good boy" followed by "good Frisbee". Follow the return with another light game of tug and a "drop" command. It is important not to pull your dog on the lead where it becomes a tug of war match. Use short pull and release motions to guide him back to you if he hesitates. Graduate from sliding the disc to rolling the disc away from you. Never let him walk away with the disc, he always needs to return it. When he does, always lavish him with praise.

Keep these games enthusiastic, fun and short. Puppies have particularly short attention spans; we don't want him getting bored with the game. We want to quit while our Patterdale still wants to play. We are teaching him that this is the greatest game in the world and that it is a special game only to be played with us. We find hallways excellent areas for these early practice sessions. You can close all the doors so he can't go anywhere, and you can make the hallway longer or shorter by adjusting where you sit in relation to the back wall.

To get your dog ready for catching discs in the air, you'll want to get him facing the proper direction to chase down the Frisbee. If you're right handed you'll want him to come towards you on your right side, go around you, and face the same direction as you on your left side. The opposite is true if you're left handed. This way when you throw the Frisbee he'll be facing the correct direction and will be able to see the disc and track it down. To train this habit, we'll teach our Pat the "around" command. This is a simple command. With some treats in your hand, have your dog sit facing you. Next, use the command "around" and lead him behind your body from right to left with the treat. Give him his treat when he comes from behind you on your left side. Very quickly your Patterdale will learn what the "around" command means.

Now that you have this training tool in place, you can begin to incorporate it into your play. Go to your hallway (or another enclosed area) with the Frisbee and your terrier. Tell your dog "around" and lead him around you with the Frisbee. When he comes up the other side, roll the Frisbee so he chases it down. As he comes back towards you with the Frisbee, again repeat the "around" command with the same action. With practice, he'll know that when he comes to you what he should do and will anticipate it.

Figure 64: "Nogger", taken in May 2014 in the hills of Hochsträss in Ulm, Germany. Photograph used with permission by Ralph Rückert.

Finally we'll start throwing the Frisbee as he comes near us. Before you start throwing the disc it's important that your dog has his adult teeth in, so he should be at least six months of age before we start these drills. Begin with short throws, gradually getting longer with successful catches. Soon we'll need to move our exercise outside (although make certain he's coming back with the disc routinely before you start adding distractions). Also we are assuming that you have a good ability to throw a Frisbee yourself. If you aren't comfortable throwing a Frisbee, this is a great activity to play with other humans for practice before working with your Pat. Once you and your Patterdale get skilled at throwing and retrieving discs, you can advance to tricks. There are some great books and videos for dog disc training. *Frisbee Dogs: How to Raise, Train, and Compete (Bloeme, 1994)* by Peter Bloeme is a great reference if you intend on pursuing this great sport with your Patterdale.

"If you've got it, flaunt it"

Mel Brooks

Figure 65: "Voodoo" wins "Under 1-Year Champion" in June 2010
at the PTCA Nationals in Gray, TN, USA.

[11]

Showing and Conformation

WE WERE NEW MEMBERS of the Dogwood Jack Russell Terrier Club in Atlanta when Voodoo joined our family (at the time of this writing, in the U.S. there are no local Patterdale Terrier clubs). We enjoy being part of a club and connecting on a regular basis with dog lovers like ourselves. We love socializing our dogs and training them on events such as racing and go-to-ground. One particular day the club was holding a training event. We brought all of our dogs along with Voodoo, our newest family member. We had fun introducing our spry, four-legged friend to lure coursing and racing. While we were passing some time splashing with the dogs in a pool, a Jack Russell Terrier Club of America (JRTCA) judge offered to give a beginning conformation lesson to any newbies at the event. I have never been comfortable being in front of crowds and therefore had never taken any interest in conformation; but my daughter asked if she could take Voodoo over to the group of trainees forming. Of course I consented. It's always nice when your five-year-old shows interest in something productive and has less fear to try something new than yourself. Our instructor was wonderful and patient with everyone there. She educated the novice handlers on how to walk and present their dogs. As the lesson came to a close, I gathered up my daughter and new pup. Our educator asked if we were entering an upcoming conformation event in a neighboring state. I smiled and simply said that conformation was not something we had planned to get involved with. The judge looked at me square in the face and said, "You have to show this dog". I was a little taken back by this forward attitude and asked her why. She responded, "I know he's still young, and his back legs are loose because he's in a growth spurt, but aside from that, he shows very nicely". I smiled, thanked her and went about the rest of the fun activities for the day.

It wasn't until much later that afternoon when we got home that I began thinking more about what the judge had said. Should we show Voodoo? What did that mean anyway? Would I have to dress up in a suit and prance around a ring in front of a crowd of people? My daughter seemed to really take an interest in exhibiting him. We were both a little shy at the time (sadly I was 37 and she was 5) but I decided that it was important for her (and her mother) to develop the skill of being comfortable in front of other people. In the end I knew this would be a great mother-daughter bonding opportunity and would help me overcome my own stage fright fears. So, we got to work training Voodoo and Carrabelle (one of our rescue Terrier mixes) at home.

Several months later we transported ourselves to Gray, Tennessee. It was the 2010 Tennessee Terrier Olympics and the Patterdale Terrier Club of America (PTCA) Nationals. Somehow my life's choices had led me to this, my first dog show, as an active participant. To add a little interest to our arrival, Carrabelle escaped. She darted out of the car, past the attendees, out of the park and straight down the highway past a group of Marines taking their morning jog. Our first dog show started off with an embarrassing escape. Fortunately, everyone there had been in our shoes at one time or another, and was happy to help retrieve our excited pup. Maybe this wouldn't be so bad after all?

Our family was having a wonderful time meeting Patterdale owners from around the nation, competing in events and socializing. Our dogs were having a great time participating in racing, running lure, going-to-ground, and barn hunt. Everyone was so friendly, as we all shared a common bond with these wonderful canine companions.

When it came time to enter my first conformation ring, I was a little uneasy. I was exhibiting Voodoo for the first time in public and he was only four months of age. John Broadhurst, a well-respected terrierman, was the judge. I did my best to present Voodoo, which included almost tripping on him while we walked around the ring. We then stood before the crowd and waited for John to make his decision. John walked over to me and extended his hand. "Oh no", I thought. "What had I done wrong?" I assumed I was allowed to use treats. Confused, I extended my treat-free hand, making for an awkward shake. That's when I realized - we had won! As he handed me the big beautiful ribbon, I just stared dumbfounded. The competition that day was tough and included two of Voodoo's littermate sisters. Being new to all of this, I wasn't sure what I was doing. I certainly thought my dog was beautiful, but don't all proud moms?

The next day was the PTCA (Patterdale Terrier Club of America) 2010 Nationals. Voodoo competed once again for Best Puppy with a new judge and finished with "Under 1-Year Champion". This put him in the final demonstration of Best Patterdale in Show. Much to my surprise and delight, we also walked away with "Best in Show Reserve" (which is the runner up for Best in Show). High on our Patterdale's success, we knew then that this was something that we should continue.

BREEDING ROOTS

Canine conformation events are derived from breeding shows of livestock (a.k.a. stock shows). In these breeding stock displays animals such as cows, swine, goats, and the like are paraded in front of ranchers who inspect them with an eye toward purchasing the offspring of animals that meet their criteria. With that in mind, we can see how showing and conformation can be dangerous in working dog breeds. If these canine conformation shows lead to the selection of breeding stock, as they quite often do in large registries, they encourage the breeding of visual attributes over work ethic. Breeding practices based on conformation weaken the work vigor of a working dog line and almost always result in caricatures of a once great type. A Patterdale Terrier should not be judged by how he looks but what he does. There is no question that this is the true measure of a great Patterdale.

The wonderful thing about our little dogs, at this time, is that most large registries don't recognize them. This keeps the Patterdale in the hands of working people that understand which dogs should be bred – those that can work! Now all that being said, it is fun to gather with other Patterdale aficionados and show off our dogs. We are all very proud Patterdale parents after all. Showing our dog is a fun bonding experience for you and your Patterdale and it often times results in you meeting like-minded interesting people and their dogs.

Exhibiting your Patterdale can be a fun family activity too. Each member of the family can have some meaningful task at a show: brushing, walking, handling or just applauding their Patterdale while he's in the ring. The children may decide to enter Junior Handler classes, while Mom or Dad can show him in other classes. The outcome of all this preparation is about two minutes in front of the judge in the ring. What precedes this moment is a great amount of knowledge, care, time and practice.

Figure 66: Skylar Miller (at age 5) shows "Voodoo" at the Middle Georgia
Kennel Club's UKC show in September 2010 in Perry, GA, USA.

Preparing your dog for a show requires that he learn good manners and some basic training. Your dog should know simple concepts like: how to conduct himself in the ring, how to walk properly on lead, how to handle people and crowds, and definitely the rules of when not to relieve himself. Show grounds are very noisy, crowded places; there are a lot of barking dogs. Your dog needs to be acclimated to people and noises so that he won't be frightened at these events. It is also worth noting that your Patterdale must be intact (not spayed or neutered) if you intend to show him. This relates to the original purpose of conformation shows, which was to evaluate breeding stock.

If conformation is something you have a mind to pursue, it is never too early to begin training. Early sessions should be short, just a few minutes at a time, keeping it fun for your Pat. Begin with simple duties like stacking and leash breaking. Though you may choose to train your Patterdale by yourself at home, conformation and handling classes can be beneficial for both you and your four-legged friend. The classes also serve to socialize your dog. This gets him accustomed to being around other dogs in conditions similar to what he'll find at shows. Your Patterdale may be the only dog in your household. Therefore at a show, he may be anxious or in awe of all the other dogs and people. Socialization will help him in any environment, where there may be a lot of people and pets, which may elicit an anxiety or fear response in your Patterdale. Handling classes address a variety of skills and potential issues and will help get your terrier ready to deal with strange people and other dogs.

If you have a new puppy, he will be able to start attending obedience and handling classes at 10 to 12 weeks of age and should be healthy and vaccinated to ensure the well-being and safety of all dogs in his class. You will most likely need to have your puppy's favorite treats with you for lessons, as well as the show lead you have chosen to use. Your instructor may have suggestions for you as to what types are typically used for Patterdale Terriers in your area.

If you are interested in showing your Patterdale it is a good idea to find a mentor. Most likely if you join a local terrier group there will be members who do regularly show their dogs and can guide you. In our area, there are significant number of breeders and handlers for Jack Russell Terriers that are always willing to offer advice and assistance. If for some reason you can't find a mentor, or you want to prepare by yourself, ideally you'll be able to start working with your puppy before he hits the six-month mark.

There are a few considerations to keep in mind if you have a puppy. First of all, be gentle with your puppy during training. You do not want to startle or scare your pup while schooling, as it can cause a bad impression of showing overall for your dog. Secondly, offer praise and encouragement, as your puppy deserves it. Praise him as soon as the he does something right to show your puppy that he is doing things correctly. Thirdly, train your puppy in small, frequent sessions. Breaking your routine up into 10 minutes sessions a couple of times a day will keep your puppy interested and avoid boredom. Lastly, never physically punish your pup. Negative reinforcement can make your puppy skittish and fearful.

Begin by spending time stacking the puppy every day and get him used to being handled and groomed. Stacking is the act of standing your pup properly to best show off his conformation and features. Patterdale Terriers are stacked with all four feet square and even, which acts to firm up your dog's build and physical characteristics. Begin preparation for stacking with your puppy at home. Put your pup on a lead and begin touching his feet gently with your hands. Pick up each foot, move it around a bit and replace it, offering your furry student a treat or toy when he stands still. Do this often to assure your pup is comfortable being handled. While stacking in competition, the judge will touch and evaluate your puppy, checking his build and teeth. You can prepare you fuzzy friend for this by having a stranger gently run his or her hands over your pup and pulling back his gums to see his teeth. Praise and talk to your puppy to reassure him to let him know it's OK to be handled, and eventually the stacking and handling will not even phase your pup.

Gaiting, or moving your puppy around the ring, is a part of showing that can make or break your day. Your dog should be gaited to display his best qualities and structural features. The proper pace is vital to a good gait. Most gaits involve a dog moving at a brisk trot, which will straighten out and strengthen the topline, and allow your dog to have the best flowing movement possible. The topline is the outline of your canine from the withers (the point on the dog's shoulders that is highest) to the point where his tail meets his backside.

Figure 67: " Shamus" is demonstrating a good "gait".
Photo taken at the 2009 PTCA Nationals in Ione, CA, USA.
Photograph used with permission by Anglo-American Patterdales.

If you want to practice gaiting, put your Patterdale on his show lead and give a command such as "let's walk" or "let's go". Begin slowly walking and then move up to a comfortable jog, encouraging your terrier to move along with you. You can play with the speed a bit to determine which speed is right for you and your dog. Once you find that pace you will always want to gait at that same speed. Praise and encourage your dog when he performs well. Showing in the conformation ring should be a fun experience for both you and your Pat.

Socialization is essential for showing your Patterdale Terrier. He should experience as many new sights, sounds, people, and dogs as possible. You should also practice grooming him. Again, start with short sessions, working on his nails, trimming his tail, ears and flanks.

When your pup gets older, he can benefit from conditioning for showing. For some dogs, this means a strict exercise regimen. For other dogs, it simply means regular walks. Some handlers have a treadmill for their dogs, ensuring proper regular exercise regardless of what the weather may be like outdoors. Nutrition is also essential to a successful show dog. A good diet and the right foods will keep your dog fit and trim, and keep his coat shining and strong.

Another thing to step-up as your puppy gets older is his education. Many obedience clubs offer drop-in conformation classes, which will give you a feel for what happens in the ring, and will get your Pat used to paying attention to you while being around other dogs and people. We should mention that there are often professional handlers in big dog shows. Professional handlers are more experienced, and are coached to bring out the best in a dog. Showing your Patterdale yourself takes a lot of hard work, patience, and a thick skin; but the bond the two of you will build during the process certainly makes it a worthy goal. It's nice to begin by showing your Patterdale as a puppy. The judges in puppy classes are much more forgiving of puppy manners and handler errors.

Once you have decided to show your Patterdale, it is worth going to a few dog shows as a spectator. Watching how it all works can make you feel more comfortable when the spotlight is on you and your dog. As a first step you'll need to find out when and where the shows are. For Patterdale Terriers there are several options for showing your dog. Those options will depend on the registries where your dog has been recorded. In the United States, the two largest registries, at the time of this writing, are the United Kennel Club (UKC) and the Patterdale Terrier Club of America (PTCA). There are UKC events and there are PTCA events. Although both similar in the way the show rings run, the events themselves are different in expectation and setting.

UKC events are much larger events with numerous dog breeds. You may be able to show your dog several times a day, and over several days meaning you could be up for a lot of walks around the ring. UKC shows are a little more formal, and you can expect to see some handlers garbed in suits or dresses.

PTCA events are smaller and occur in lower frequency. Generally there is at least one conformation show held each year at differing locales around the United States. The PTCA Nationals, the biggest show for the PTCA, awards championship (CH) titles based on the judge's decision for the Patterdale that best fits the breed standard for each category (i.e. Best Male, Best Female, Best Puppy, etc.). Field Championships are awards based on merit. Candidates are monitored through working observations of other terriermen. Exceptional working ability is considered. Because of the working nature of this breed, the events tend to be more casual in dress.

Once you have found a show and submitted your entries, it's time to think about what you're going to need for your first dog show. It's best to start putting items together, so you won't forget something important. Make sure you have done your homework and know everything you will need to bring to your first show. Of course, you will need a show lead for your dog. For our terriers, nylon is a good option. It's the least expensive and is the gentlest on his neck. The collar is placed high on the neck, right behind his ears, and should only have an inch or two of extra collar when it is fit snugly. Appropriate colors for nylon are white, black, or brown. The general train of thought is to make the lead invisible, not to draw attention to it. So if you have a black Patterdale a thin black nylon show lead is a good choice.

By getting a lead that is the same color as your dog you will make your Pat's neck look longer. Much like when humans wear a belt, it can visually cut us in half at the middle. It is recommended to use a special dog show collar and lead, called a Martingale. It is both a collar and lead in one that allows for you to adjust the collar right at the neck to appropriately control your terrier's head. Let your dog know that this is a "special" collar by using it sparingly and with enthusiasm and praise when he walks appropriately while wearing it.

Figure 68: A Patterdale wears a Martingale collar at the
Gold Coast Terrier Trial in February 2014 in Bronson, FL, USA.

Another item that you will definitely need to bring is his crate. This is especially important if you will be at the show for a majority of the day. Don't think that you can just hold on to your dog or keep them tied up if they will be in classes at various times throughout the day. Prior to and after each class he enters, you will want to put him back in his crate to rest. Make sure he is hydrated and that the inside of his crate is comfortable. You may want to lay a blanket or towel on the top of the crate to block from view any people or dogs that might pass by. Don't find out the hard way that your dog was disqualified because he was stressed.

Other items to bring with you are small towels to clean up your dog's feet and coat before you enter the ring. A soft dog brush isn't a bad idea either. You will also need to bring food and water bowls and cleanup bags. Be sure to also have your dog's registration and health records with you.

What can you expect at a Patterdale Conformation show? There are specific list of items that the judges will be looking at when evaluating your Patterdale. You want to make sure you are prepared to accent your dogs' best features. There are several things to consider before entering the ring.

First, make certain your Martingale lead is on properly and held correctly by you. Slip the head hole of the lead gently over your Pats head. There is a small clasp that you can adjust how loose or how tight you want it to be. You want it to be snug and positioned as close to the dogs jaw as possible. You want it to be reasonably tight so that it will not move from this position. If you can control your dog's head, you can control your dog. This will also help keep his head held upward and looking at you.

Once the dog is positioned on the lead, it's time for you to present yourself. The best way to use your leash in the ring is to scrunch up your leash in your hand by folding it up to make it disappear. You want your leash held in your hand to be at waist height. This creates a neat presentation. The elbow of your arm holding the lead should be at a 90-degree angle. You will want to make sure that you are keeping your dog on a short leash. This will give you maximum control and ensure that your dog does not wander.

Have your Patterdale walk at your knee, or as close to it as he will get. You want to make sure that he will walk fast enough so that he will be not distracted by scents or other diversions that may catch his attention on the floor, if he has the time to look. You can give him short and gentle "pops" upward when his head gets close to the floor, if you need to. If he becomes distracted, make sure to hold his lead higher up on his neck as to position his head upward and away from the floor. Be careful not to hold him too high up, you don't want his feet to be lifted from the floor.

Your goal should be focused on showing his motion to the judges. They want to see him trot. One exercise you can practice at home is to walk with your Patterdale from one end of your driveway (or similar length) to the other end. Do this repeatedly and he will eventually get bored and more likely to pay attention to you.

In the ring, you will want to make sure that your Patterdale is alert and attentive to your words and direction. Find a word that will focus his mind on you. "Watch" and "focus" are common choices. It is acceptable, especially if he is a puppy, to stop and get him to focus and then begin your walk again. At one point in your walk around the ring, a judge will direct you to "stop". At this time you are going to want your dog to stand "square". Put him in a stand position, with his feet at all points of the square. Think about a square, or more of a rectangle that is between all four of your dog's feet. You can practice this at home with a treat, work with him to get him in the square position, and then reward him. You may want to associate a word like "stand" with this position and repeat it when he gets his reward.

Learn what the best feature of your dog is. You want the judge to see this part of your dog. For example if the best feature of your dog is his face you don't want his back-end facing the judge. You want him looking at you, with his tail up showing that he is alert. Having a tail pointing down will indicate that he is afraid and not paying attention. Vicious and extremely shy dogs will be disqualified.

When the judge comes over she will ask you how old your dog is. She will walk to either the center or side of the ring and ask you to have the dog walk towards her. She will look at his teeth. She will check his coat. For male dogs, she will make sure his reproductive organs are intact and come in a pair. She will check his flexibility. She will check that he has all of his toes.

Sometimes she will ask you to walk in a pattern. What you should hold in mind is that it is your job to keep the dog between you and the judge. In this way, she can see the dog coming towards her, going away, and see him from the side. Don't let your Patterdale pull. If he is pulling give him a quick and gentle "pop" or pull upwards on his lead. If you let him pull, he will continue to do it and it will become a habit for him. You should make him understand at a young age that pulling is not acceptable. If your dog is an excessive puller, you may want to consider employing a pinch collar during training. This is a safe and effective collar that gently pinches your Pat's skin and hair when tension is on the leash. Used appropriately, it can be an effective learning tool to teach a dog to stop pulling on walks. A head halter is another option, which discourages pulling by pointing his face towards you.

After the judge has looked at all of the dogs, she will have you take one more walk around the ring, to check her notes, and see each dog one more time. The judge will form a conclusion about how the dog's build and movement all came together and if your Patterdale can truly perform the functions for which he was bred. The judge will then make her final decision. Typically, the judge will hand out the ribbons in place order, or pull a couple of the dogs for one final review.

It is important for you to know exactly what the judge is looking for in a conformation event. For all registered dogs there is a written standard. Although most are similar, be sure to consult the breed standard that best matches the show you are attending. This standard outlines the outward attributes of a dog breed in relation to the duties it is expected to perform. As such, the appearance of the dog will relate to the functions it is expected to perform. Every Patterdale judge is required to know the history of the breed and what he was bred to do to best. They will understand how form and function must come together in the show ring. They must also know the Patterdale standard. At Patterdale conformation shows, although the dog doesn't get the opportunity to actually perform his duties in the ring, the judge must envision the dog doing so by analyzing his form.

The breed standards have very specific guidelines about the looks and movement of the Patterdale Terrier. The Patterdale is a working terrier, bred originally to go to ground and kill or bolt quarry. This requires a small, active, game terrier that is not big in the chest, and is capable of squeezing through very small passages underground. The dog should present a compact, balanced image, but should never appear short backed or cobby, meaning that they are short and compact. A little long in body will be better accepted than a dog too tall or too cobby. The head should be balanced with the size of the dog. Dogs should be shown in a hard, fit working condition, with no excess fat.

Generally, a Patterdale's weight should be in proportion to height and within a range of 10 to 17 pounds. The ideal Patterdale Terrier is a working terrier that will go-to-ground, seeking out his prey. Patterdales are very active and have a strong prey drive. The head should be in balance to the body, and should be strong and powerful.

Teeth should be strong, meeting in a scissor or level bite. The judge might ask you what type of bite the dog has and your answer should always be "scissor". The canines (the four pointed teeth that are located next to the incisors on each side of both the upper and lower jaw right) should be broad based and tapered to the end. The incisors are the sharp edged teeth used for cutting or gnawing that are found between the canines and consisting of the six upper and six lower front teeth that form the point of contact in a bite. Dogs that have broken canines or missing incisors due to working are not to be penalized.

A Patterdale should have a strong neck. This is as important as a strong jaw in killing prey. The neck should blend smoothly into the shoulders with tight fitting skin giving a clean appearance. A neck that is too short or too thick may have points deducted. One of the most important attributes of a Patterdale Terrier is a flexible chest that can be spanned. A small, compressible, properly shaped chest will allow the dog to move and enter the ground. Having a flexible chest sets the Patterdale apart from the other terrier breeds and insures that he will be able to function as an earth-working terrier. Spanning is an important part of the judging process for a go-to-ground terrier. It will look like the judge is giving the dog a hug when they lift the front legs off of the ground and gently squeeze the bottom of the chest to be certain that the chest will compress.

The tail should be held high. A high tail expresses confidence; a lowered tail or a tail between the legs expresses fear. If the tail is docked, only a quarter to a third should be removed. The tail should be strong, but not overly thick or carried over the back.

What color is your Patterdale? You might be asked this question and you don't want to get it wrong. Acceptable Patterdale colors are black, red, chocolate (previously known as liver), grizzle, black and tan, and bronze (black that shines bronze/brown in the sunlight, also known as seal or blue). The nose should be black except for chocolate-colored dogs, which have a red nose. Chocolate dogs may have amber colored eyes; all other colors should have dark brown eyes. Patterdales are solid in color. Any white markings will be confined to the chest and feet. Points will be deducted if your Patterdale has white markings other than the chest and feet.

Another question you might be asked is what type of coat your Patterdale has. Get familiar with the different types so you have the right answer. The coat of a Patterdale can be smooth, broken, or rough. The coats of all Patterdale terriers should be thick and dense. This is critical to protect them against the wet, cold underground, underbrush and briars. A "smooth" coat is dense and stiff (no waves), and will fall back in place when lifted. You will not see facial hair on a smooth coated dog. A "broken" coat is an intermediate coat having longer guard hairs over the face or body. A broken coated dog may or may not have facial hair. The coat over the body is stiff and dense. Lastly, a "rough" coat may be slightly wiry but not overly stiff. Facial and body hair will be like the base coat of the body. On both the broken and rough coat a slight wave is allowed.

Throughout your showing career remember to have fun and smile. The dogs that are the most successful are the ones having fun, and they can sense your energy if you are tense or upset. If you're happy, the dog will be happy. You can overcome tension by spending time with your Patterdale at home practicing.

All show dogs need to be clean – with clean teeth and clean, trimmed toenails. As this breed has a short coat, minimal grooming is needed to keep the Patterdale Terrier in tip-top shape. The night before the show, you may want to give your Patterdale a bath and groom him. Brushing with a firm bristle or rubber brush will remove excess hair. Patterdales love to dig so be sure to clean his feet. For the Patterdale, all you will need to do is trim away any long hairs. It seems like a small thing, but it can really clean up his outline. And last but not least, try to get a good night's sleep. Feeling refreshed will keep your spirits high as you make your way around the ring. Good luck and have fun!

"Dogs feel very strongly that they should always go with you in the car, in case the need should arise for them to bark violently at nothing right in your ear."

Dave Barry

Figure 69: Your Patterdale will enjoy going on adventures with you.
Be prepared, and it will be enjoyable for everyone!
"Zinger" taken in April 2014 in Ruskin, FL, USA.
Photograph used with permission by Anglo-American Patterdales.

[12]

Travel

WHEN I MET MY HUSBAND he came with a sweet and loving American Pit Bull Terrier named Moses. Moses was many things. But perhaps foremost topping that list, Moses was an impassioned automobile cruising devotee. The mere utterance of the word "ride" by anyone in the house initiated a mad dash towards the door with subsequent hysterical whining and concentrated glaring at the kitchen doorknob. As soon as that door opened, he would make a beeline for the car. Once the car door was released, he would leap into the passenger seat and plant his butt down smiling ear-to-ear, ready to cruise.

Moses loved to ride in the car so much that often times we would take him on short rides to the grocery store or the like, just to make him happy. He would sit in the front seat and poke his nose at the window pleading for you to roll it down for him. If you did, he reached a state of complete bliss. He would thrust his noggin' directly out the window, head held high, ears flapping in the wind. Sometimes the wind would catch under his eyelids and sides of his mouth creating this crazy, cartoonish, caricature of his face. It was truly a sight to behold.

Moses was a very intelligent soul. He was smart enough to know that if we left the house, we had gone with the car. He didn't know where we went or when we would return, but somehow the car was related to our adventures outside of the home. One evening after work, Mick and I ran out to grab a meal and run some errands. As we pulled into the driveway, the headlights of my car illuminated a most peculiar sight. There was Moses (all 65 pounds of him) seated in the driver side of Mick's car. His head was sticking out the window and he was looking at us with an expression that said, "What took you so long? I'm ready to ride!" Moses had apparently leapt over the fence and managed to jump in through the open window of the car. To him, it was the ticket to ride. Some dogs like to travel – *a lot.*

SAFETY FIRST

We hesitated including this story as it does demonstrate that we had some bad travel habits with Moses. We are much better at addressing safety first when we travel with our canine companions today. Traveling means different things to different people. Some people relish travel and live for seeing new sights and experiencing new environments. Others prefer the comfort found in their own neighborhood, with friends and family they've grown to love. Regardless of each individual's feelings on the matter, chances are high that most of us will need to get behind the wheel of a car or jump on a plane at some point in our lives. Many times we will have the option to bring along our favorite furry companion with us. Our Patterdale is part of our family, and it is usually fun to include him in our adventures, whether that trip is a short car ride to the local park or a cross-country adventure.

Planning is the key to a successful, enjoyable trip with your terrier. Whether you are traveling by car or plane, staying in a hotel or camping, a little planning will make the experience a positive one. So before traveling by land, air, or water let's make sure we go through a suitable doggie checklist.

First and foremost, we need to make sure our friend has identification. Make certain his ID tag is firmly secured to his collar and that it has your current mobile phone number (you're travelling too remember). It is also a good idea to bring a recent photo of your Patterdale in the event he gets lost on your trip. Of course, you can't forget his lead. While away from your home your dog should always be on a leash. Remember he is in unfamiliar territory and won't know his way back home if he gets separated from you.

Second, make sure your Patterdale Terrier is current on all his vaccinations before you take him on an excursion. Bring his shot records with you in case you need to provide proof to any authorities. Keep in mind that while travelling, your dog will come in contact with new environments, new dogs and new people. You need to protect him as well as those around you. In addition, your Vet's number should be saved on your phone or written and retained in your wallet should you need it.

Third, a crate is recommended for safety. It is a good way to keep your Patterdale safe in the car and is required if you will be boarding an airplane. It can also be a good way to keep your pet out of trouble if you are staying at a hotel or a friend's house and want to go out for a bit and leave your terrier at home. When in unfamiliar places an unsupervised canine can get anxious and cause a good bit of trouble. Your Pat's crate is his safe cave of comfort and will help keep him at ease and out of trouble when you can't watch him. Keep a blanket from home in his crate to keep him calm and be absorbent in the case of an accident.

Fourth, keeping a first aid kit with you is a good idea. A few items to include in your kit are a topical antibiotic for cuts and bruises, gauze and wrapping tape, and tweezers for removing splinters or ticks. If your dog takes any other medication make sure you bring that too. See the chapter on Healthcare and Grooming for more specifics on what to include in your first aid kit.

Make certain that your destination is pet friendly. If you are staying at a hotel ask what amenities are available to your dog, and also ask the cost. Many hotels charge a non-refundable pet fee and sometimes an additional daily pet fee. Many have size or breed restrictions as well. Make sure that the front desk knows that your dog is there and notifies the staff. In addition, if you do need to leave make sure to put a "Do Not Disturb" sign on the door so that housekeeping won't be alarmed to find a barking dog when they open the door. The bottom line is to do your homework on the place that you pick out to make sure it is a good fit for you and your Patterdale.

Now we need to consider our mode of transportation. When traveling by car, we will want our Patterdale Terrier to travel in his crate. Our terriers are energetic little beasts and if left to their own devices in an automobile they will distract us, which can cause dire results. As an illustrative story, I once hopped in the car to pick up my daughter from a neighbor's house. My Patterdale Terrier, Voodoo, raced into the vehicle after me. I thought, "Oh I'm just running down the street, he'll be fine". This is a decision I would soon come to regret. As soon as the car began moving he began bounding around the vehicle like a complete spaz. It was at this moment when I remembered why it's so important to crate him. By the time I had reached the end of the block I heard honking behind me. I stopped the car. A neighbor came out of his sedan behind me to tell me my dog had just jumped out of the window. Sure enough, my little Voodoo had stepped on the power window button, rolled down the window and leapt out of the car. Fortunately Voodoo was fine, running around, just as proud as he could be of himself, chasing squirrels. But I shudder to think what would have happened if I had been driving down the interstate. Your Patterdale Terrier will grow to enjoy crate travel. Whenever our dogs see us taking the crates to the car they spring up and down with excitement. They can't wait to get in and go for a ride.

If we're taking a long road trip we'll need to do additional pre-trip planning. Besides just bringing along his crate, we need to make sure we plan to stop every 4 hours or so to allow our furry friend to get a drink of water and relieve himself. We don't want our canine companion to have an accident in the car. It's a good time to stretch our legs as well. It is also wise to identify a veterinarian in the area we're visiting just in case of an emergency. Be sure to pack a travel bag for your dog and keep it handy in the car. Make certain you are able to easily access the contents of his bag, particularly his leash. Bring a large bottle of water and a water bowl. Pack some treats in the event that your dog wanders off and you need something enticing to lure him back. If your dog likes to chew (and what Patterdale doesn't?) bring several chew toys. Don't forget biodegradable bags to pick up waste. If you are uncertain that your destination will have your brand of food, be sure to bring enough for the whole trip.

Figure 70: "Beag", taken in May 2014 at
Fountainstown Beach in East County Cork, Ireland.
Photograph used with permission by Liam O Shea.

Always book hotel accommodations in advance, as there may be a limited number of pet friendly rooms. When possible, request a room on the first floor so that if your dog needs to go out frequently it won't be too far of a walk. Camping is also great way to spend time with your dog while communing with nature. What is a more perfect setting for a traveling dog than the great outdoors? This is not to say that there won't be challenges so again, plan ahead. Patterdales are known to chase any piece of fur that moves and skunks, raccoons, and other wildlife can bite or otherwise injure your dog. Make sure they are always within sight and on a leash. If the campground will allow it, stakeouts are a great way to keep your dog outside but nearby. Make sure your dog is up to date on flea and tick medication and is vaccinated against rabies. Carry an adequate supply of water for both you and your dog. Many campgrounds allow dogs, but some do not so it is always wise to check on policies before you arrive. In the U.S., many state and national parks do not allow dogs.

While travelling, keep your car well ventilated and make certain air can flow through his crate. If you are traveling in the summer, air conditioning is a must. If the weather is nice, it is perfectly fine to keep your windows down while traveling. It is not safe however to let your dog ride with his head sticking out of the window. This can lead to particles of dirt, rocks or other debris from the road flying into his eyes, ears, and/or nose, causing serious injury or infection. It should be obvious that you never let your dog ride in the back of an open truck. Any bump in the road could launch him into the road and would most certainly be disastrous. If your dog must ride in the back of a truck make sure he is confined in a protective kennel that is fastened securely to the truck bed.

Never leave your dog unattended in a closed car, especially in the summer. Like people, dogs can get overheated. Dogs sweat through their mouth. Unlike humans who perspire through their arms and other appendages, dogs pant. If they are panting hard, let them drink water, dip them in water, or find them a cool place to lie down. Overheating is a serious problem, especially for our little black dogs that absorb a great deal of sunlight.

Just like humans, dogs can get motion sickness. One way to avoid this is to arrange for him to travel on an empty stomach. This applies to food only. You will want to make sure that there is water available to him. When it is time to make stops, try to avoid busy rest stops. Not only can they dangerous with so many cars coming and going, but also you can't be certain about other unvaccinated dogs they may be there. Whenever possible try to find quiet rest areas to stop.

While most dogs love car travel (particularly our headstrong, fearless Patterdale Terriers) in a few animals it may be a source of anxiety. If you find your furry friend to fall in this category, we need to build up his confidence and comfort with vehicles. This would include opening the car and putting him and his crate in the car with the door open. Give him a treat to let him know that its O.K. Repeat this exercise once a day until he gets comfortable that nothing is going to happen to him. Then change the exercise to include closing the car door. Again, give him a treat to console him. Now that he's comfortable sitting in his crate with you in a closed car, let's graduate to movement. Turn on the car, and give him a treat. Turn off the car. Repeat exercises until ease is seen in your terrier. Next we'll slowly move down the driveway, and then take a trip around the block. Finally take short trips that end positively (like to the park). It's all about baby steps and positive associations. Before you know it, your dog will have no problem with car rides and actually look forward to them.

If you are traveling via airplane you will need to perform some alternate preparations. Each airline has specific rules for traveling dogs so we need to make sure to check their specific policies and procedures. As a rule, all airlines will require health certifications and proof of vaccinations. In addition, dogs less than 8 weeks old are not allowed to travel and pregnant and older dogs are discouraged from flying.

When travelling with your dog on an airplane there are three ways he can travel. One, if your Patterdale is small enough you may be allowed to carry them onboard in a carrier. To qualify your terrier must be small enough to fit in a kennel without touching the sides and with the ability to move around. This kennel must fit under the seat in front of you. Most airlines will count your pet as a piece of carry-on luggage and in addition will charge you a pet travel fee.

The second means of having your pet travel on a plane is as checked baggage. If he will be travelling by this route he will need a hard sided travel carrier. Of course there is still a pet baggage fee and you must be on the same flight as your Patterdale. Make sure whenever travelling this way to do your best to make his kennel comfortable with soft blankets, toys, and treats.

The third way of your dog travelling via plane is as cargo. Often with airlines, there is no guarantee as to which flight your dog will be on if they fly as cargo. Depending on the time of year, some airlines will not transport animals when it is extremely hot or cold for the safety of your pet. In addition, when travelling as cargo some airlines require a water dish to be attached to the kennel, in case there is a delay and airline staff needs to provide water to your pet.

When traveling by plane, always try to book a direct flight. This will help make sure that your dog isn't stuck in his crate any longer than he needs to be. It is also helpful to book the flight as far in advance as possible as there is usually a limit as to the number of dogs permitted on each flight. You will be responsible for purchasing a separate ticket for your dog, the details of which is specific to the airline carrier. Reconfirm your flight the day prior to your departure to make sure that there have been no last minute changes.

On the day of the flight, take your dog for a walk. Make sure that he has had a little bit of exercise prior to traveling. Arrive at the airport early. Make sure you are the one that puts your dog in the crate and gives it a little positive reinforcement. When you board the plane tell a member of the flight crew that your pet is in the cargo hold. If you are able to travel with your dog in the cabin, arrange to check in as late as possible to reduce the amount of time that they will have to spend at the airport. You may be asked to remove your pet from the carrier so that the carrier can be put through an x-ray scanner. Make sure that your Patterdale has a collar attached with identification even when in the crate.

If you are thinking about purchasing a crate there are a few things to keep in mind. First of all, select a crate that is large enough to allow the dog to stand, turn around, and lie down. You will also want to make sure that the bottom of the crate is leak proof. Make sure it is properly ventilated on opposing sides. If you will be putting the crate on an airplane make sure that it is labeled "Live Animal" and has your name, address, and phone number where you can be reached during your travels.

Travel by train and bus is not generally allowed. Amtrak trains and Greyhound buses do not allow dogs. Depending on the state you live in you may be able to take your dog on a local railway. Check with your local and state guidelines to see if dogs are allowed. No matter where your travels may take you, remember to always plan ahead. A little planning can go a long way in making your trip more enjoyable for everyone involved.

"The difference between what we do and what we are capable of doing would suffice to solve most of the world's problem."

Mohandas Karamchand Ghandi

Figure 71: "Milo", taken in the spring of 2015 in a cornfield near Towcester, UK.
Photograph used with permission by Tex Marshall.

[13]

Some Green Notes...

THE GREEN MOVEMENT isn't anything new. It has been around for decades. One of the first books to shine a light on our increased exposure to toxins was "Silent Spring" by Rachel Carson in 1962. Rachel detailed that poisons from insecticides, agricultural sprays and other common products were entering our food supply. She went on to point out that we are exposed to toxins that stay in our bodies throughout our entire lives. This is certainly not the most pleasant of discussion topics. The good news, for our pets and us, is that there is more and more attention being focused on food safety and dangerous chemicals in today's society.

Great strides have been made since Carson's eye-opening book was printed and with the illumination of the damaging effects of man on his environment. Over the years, man has learned to have a more harmonious role in his environment. It is up to each one of us to care for this beautiful planet in which we live. It is easy to think that just one person's efforts won't make a difference. This broadly held belief is simply not true. We all need to take a look at our lifestyles and their impact on others from time to time. Each one of us should feel comfortable with our relationship with the environment.

Going green usually takes some effort. We're walking instead of driving and we are separating our trash for recycling. All of this takes a little extra time out of our busy lives. We are buying and preparing more fresh foods instead of buying pre-packaged ones. If you are going green with your family, you may have thought about including your dog in this earth-saving adventure. It's easy to miss the magnitude with which our furry friends play on the environment. Most of us think that its people that we need to worry about and we often tend to overlook the carbon paw print that our furry friends are leaving behind. With the number of dogs on the rise at alarming levels (unfortunately they do not all have loving homes), it is time to think about what we can do to make the world the better place for our furry companions and us.

A 2012 report from the APPA (American Pet Products Association) stated that there are 83.3 million dogs in the United States alone, with 47% of all households owning at least one dog. That number was up more than 10 million from the year before. It is hard to estimate the world dog population, but with an estimated 3,000 dogs born each hour, it is immense. With this dramatic expansion in dogs there is undoubtedly an increase in waste products into our environment. Think of all of the dog food containers, discarded plastic toys, packaging, and plastic bags used to discard pet waste. There is also the issue of pet waste itself. Where is all of it going? Well, let's just say it's not disappearing, as we would like to turn our heads and think. It is filling up landfills and causing unsafe chemicals to be emitted into the ozone, as well as into our water supply.

Now we certainly don't mean to deter you from adopting that wonderful rescue dog that needs a good home. We are simply pointing out that as we are responsible for our dogs, we are also responsible for their environmental impact. Should we all start feeding our dogs nuts and berries? No, I don't think Fido is ready to go "granola". Face the nature of our furry friends: dogs do need to eat meat. This is part of their genetic makeup. But have you checked a package of dog food lately?

Take this challenge: go to the store and try to find a bag of dog food that listed meat as the main ingredient. Chances are you will be surprised to find that there are very few options that list meat products first. Corn is often used as a filler to make the dog food cheaper for you to buy. The more corn and fillers the dogs eat, the more dog food they will consume as a whole, translating to more dog food purchases for you. Switching to a meat based dog food may be more expensive, but your dog will eat half as much. Half as much food equals half as much packaging, and half as much fuel used to produce the dog food and drive it to your local store. Look how one little thing you can do creates a major environmental impact!

As the market catches up with the demand and need for organic and green products, we pet owners can do the basic research to provide healthy and eco-friendly pet food. Start by trying to find local pet food stores that carry foods with wholesome, nutritive ingredients. If you are feeling ambitious, make your own dog food with fresh, filler-free ingredients. Choose meats that are not meat by-products. These animal by-products, otherwise known as low-grade wastes from the beef and poultry industries are used to make many dog foods on the store shelves. Many of the animals used to make various pet foods are classified as "4-D," which is really a polite way of saying "Dead, Dying, Diseased, or Down (Disabled)" when they line up at the slaughterhouse. Unless your ingredients list explicitly states that it contains FDA-certified, food-grade meat, you should know that its contents are considered unfit for human consumption, but apparently good enough for your dog. Of course the only way to truly know for sure what is in your dog's food is simply to make it yourself.

Here's the straight poop: with more fillers in dog food, dogs will also produce more waste. There are several easy and cheap options to pick up after your pet and help the environment. The ideal situation is to flush pet waste down the toilet so that it will get the same treatment as human waste. There are flushable, biodegradable poop bags available. Another option is to use biodegradable bags and toss them in the trash. At a cost of six to ten cents per bag, biodegradable cornstarch pet waste clean-up bags are an inexpensive way to help the environment. Readily available in nearby pet stores and online, they are a convenient way to help curb waste and pollution. Instead of filling the earth for up to 1,000 years, they turn into compost in 10 to 90 days. Because of shorter decomposition time, there is less likelihood of causing harm to wildlife than with the use of plastic bags. Polyethylene-free production reduces the release of unnatural hydrocarbons and carcinogens into the environment. Polyethylene is the key ingredient in plastic bags, a rising environmental issue.

Unfortunately, many pet owners are still using plastic bags to pick up pet waste. Plastic bags do not decompose and actually preserve the pet waste in the landfills. Plastic grocery bags fill landfills where they remain for up to 1000 years, harming the environment by killing marine birds, whales, seals, turtles and other mammals. When animals accidentally ingest them, the plastic bags fill their stomachs, inhibit digestion of food, and cause starvation. Animals can also die when entangled or trapped by plastic bags. At the grocery store, remember to bring your reusable bags (most stores have them available for about a dollar) or if you forget to bring them, opt for paper bags.

If you are lucky enough to live in a city where you can walk everywhere, why not kill two birds with one stone by walking your dog and running your errands? Unfortunately, we can't all do this if we aren't within walking distance to our local stores. If you are fortunate enough to be able to walk to your shopping destinations try taking your dog with you. Both you and your dog get exercise and you can leave the car at home. Everyone wins.

Consider earth friendly dog supplies. Green products are safer for your dog. An interesting note is that the pet industry has little regulation over pet toys. Pet toys have been known to contain dangerous chemicals, which can be harmful to your dog. Always read the label. If you can't find an ingredient list or chemical makeup of the toy or treat, pass it up. There are many web sites now that offer safe pet toys and treats.

Dogs need to chew; however many pet toys and chews available today are not safe and may contain chemicals that could lead to costly vet trips or even death. The best chew toy you can find is in your local butcher department: beef marrowbones. Make sure you get smaller bones for a smaller dog. There is no need to cook them, just serve them raw. Cooking may cause the bones to splinter. Marrowbones are typically a fraction of the cost of a purchased chew toy bone and can last up to a couple of months.

Any effort you can make to preserve the environment is worth doing. It's not easy to change your routine and buying choices for your dog. Take it one step at a time and do what works for you. Every little thing you can do to help preserve the future of our earth is a step in the right direction. As conscience human beings it is our responsibility to make the world a better and safer place for the generations of pets and pet owners to come.

Figure 72: "Denzil" and "Millie", photo taken in
December, 2013 on Poole Heathland in Dorset, UK.
Photograph used with permission by Gareth Dancey.

Figure 73: Andrea Marshall pictured with "Brandy".
Photo taken in October 2014 in Ruskin, FL, USA.
Photograph used with permission by Andrea Marshall.

[14]

Andrea Marshall

THERE IS NO GREATER CHAMPION of the Patterdale Terrier in North America at the time of this publishing than Andrea Marshall. We have personally known and learned a lot from Andrea over the past five years. During that time, she has shown herself to be a tireless protector and ambassador of the Patterdale Terrier type. With the help of her husband Jeremy, they have personally spearhead, coordinated, promoted, and executed every PTCA National Championship competition in the U.S. over the past five years. She is a well-respected breeder in the U.S., with her kennel Anglo-American Patterdale Terriers, and was the person we turned to when it was time to get our first (and later second) Patterdale. We personally thank Andrea for her tireless commitment to Patterdales and greatly value her friendship. We had a brief interview with Andrea to get a bit of her perspective on these wonderful little creatures.

TIRELESS PATTERDALE PROMOTER

What was your first experience with dogs?

My earliest childhood memories are all of dogs. I lived with my mom and grandparents and they raised AKC Chinese Pugs. My first dog was an amazing little Pug named "Pugsy", he was born 1 year to the day after I was. My grandparents raised a few litters and my friends and I "socialized" them for their new homes. We had several other great dogs over the years, a Boxer named Garson who was the clown of the family. I had a great German Shepard mix named "Betty" who was the queen of escapes.

It was not until I met my husband that I thought of breeding myself. I was working as a vet tech when we met. He had formerly bred American Pit Bull Terriers

(APBT) when he lived in Indiana. I had never had any real exposure to the breed, and was a little hesitant, but shortly after we moved in together we went to Indiana and picked up our first APBT, "PopTart". She was such an amazing dog; I fell in love with her instantly. "PopTart" was a terrific athlete and I wanted to find outlets for her energy. In doing so, I found a local American Dog Breeders Association (ADBA) APBT club and went to my first "dog show". I loved it because there were several events we were able to try her in: conformation, weight pull and hang time. I was hooked. This show started it all for me. I'd been raised around dogs and had already been a vet tech for several years; the wick was there I just needed it to be lit. I spent hours and hours obsessed with learning everything I could about genetics and breeding, pedigree research, conformation and trainingthen we started our APBT kennel. We actively bred and competed with APBT's for about ten years and still own one today. I ran an ADBA club for a few years, which continued to fuel my fire for competition and my respect for terrier athletes in general.

How did you become involved with Patterdales and how long you've been working with this type?

Through our ventures with the American Pit Bull Terrier I met my partner in the Patterdale Terriers, Wendy Raulerson. She had some beautiful American Pit Bull Terriers and we hit it off right away. When I went to see her yard for the first time she had some small terriers named Suzy, Bart, Maggie and Mr. Mickers (who became the foundation of what is now Anglo-American). They we're extremely cute, but the thing that stood out the most to me was the way they held their own in the yard full of APBT's. They were only about 15 pounds but they didn't know it. I'm sure Bart thought he was 150 pounds. A few months after first meeting them, I had to transition my then house dog to an outside dog because of behavior issues and did not want another big dog in the house. Wendy had just bred Suzy Q and wanted to keep her daughter Bizzy so she offered me Suzy Q. Suzy was not a people friendly dog and it took a lot to gain her trust. After about two days later I was able to touch her and spent time sitting in the yard with her. Letting her warm up to me eventually worked to a small degree. My husband and son were a different story: she went mad whenever they were around and she was very nervous. Wendy had rescued her as a young dog and she was the only one who Suzy ever really trusted so I took her back to Wendy's and Wendy let me take a Bizzy instead. Bizzy was what I call a "heart dog". She was amazing and hysterical and the most human like dog I ever owned. She won my heart in days. A new obsession started an obsession that has become my everyday life. I started doing all the research I could trying to find breeders, history, anything I could which was not much. I found the Patterdale Terrier Club of America, MQH Kennel in California and David Mason in Tennessee. I contacted the few people I could find with Patterdales and I was time and time again referred to David Mason. I called David Mason and told him I wanted a male, color and coat was unimportant. He told me he had a four-month-old male and if I could pick him up, to come and get him. I went to Tennessee two days later and brought home Shamus. Shortly after Shamus I took on my first of many "rescue" Patterdales Izabel Parks, who had been abused and her breeder could not take her back and so she was given to me. I was blessed that day; Izabel was one of my all-time "Best Friends" and the final piece that started my line of the Patterdales. Wendy and I started our Patterdale Kennel officially in May of 2002. Like Patterdales, Wendy is from England. She is the "Anglo" and I am the "American" of our kennel today. While we both focused our lines on the Vetzel/Parks dogs, we both bred and concentrated on our own crosses and we have maintained one kennel with two distinct lines of dogs. We are fortunate enough to have our lines being bred and competed all over the world.

Why do you love Patterdales so much versus other types?

There are several reasons that a Patterdale Terrier really stands out to me over other breeds. My number one love in breeds in general are terriers, I love their eagerness to please which is a typical well-bred terrier's disposition. Patterdale Terriers are extremely loyal and bond to their owner, which goes back to their eagerness to please. They are extreme athletes running the equivalent of mini strong man competitions at any trial. Their endless energy and drive, which to some can also be considered a fault, is one of the best things about them. Mostly I think it's the fact that the breed was untainted when I discovered them. They were rarely being competed with and most "breeders" were still working the stock and breeding them strictly for working. Many of the most "popular" breeds are also the most troubled breeds. When breeds become popular and easily available, everyone wants to be a breeder, everyone wants to make money and the breed becomes riddled with health and behavior issues. I believe for the most part those dedicated to the Patterdale Terrier are selective breeders. As the breed has become more popular I have seen some evidence of poor breeding and a few health issues in certain lines but for the most part the Patterdale is still a hearty, well-tempered breed.

Are there any Patterdales that have been particularly special to you?

All of my Patterdales have truly been special to me. I have a distinct purpose for my terriers: I want healthy, sound, well-tempered, eager-to-please, sociable, competitive dogs with proper conformation for working. Not every Patterdale we have worked with or produced have met those standards and have gone from our stock to pets in loving homes. If I were to keep every Patterdale I liked I'd have a million dogs and so our selection is kept to those that can do everything we expect in a well-rounded dog. I do have my "heart dogs", those that have just been a little closer to me than others. First would be Miz Bizzy, my first Patterdale, who started the craziness that is my life today. Bizzy died at just six in an accident but for those six years she was at my hip. She went to work with me, she slept in our bed, she went everywhere with us and she was never really replaced in our hearts.

UKC Ch/PTCA 3x National Veteran Champion Anglo-American's Izabel Parks COG, "Izabel" came to me when she was a little over a year old. Her breeder went by to check on her and see how she was doing with her new owners and found her living in awful conditions. At the time he could not take care of her and gave her to me. She had every type of worm, was covered in fleas and it took us almost a year to get her bowels back to normal. She was a beautiful female once we got her back into shape and she was our first Champion. Izabel loved to work, she had absolutely no fear, she was a rocket go-to-ground dog and excelled at anything we taught her. After we lost Bizzy, Izabel took the rightful place as the queen of the house and we saw her turn into an even better terrier. Izabel never met a person she didn't like and had an awesome smile. She was our nanny dog; Izabel "raised" every new dog we ever brought home or kept. Izabel would basically teach them all the rules of the house and helped potty train. She kept order, if they got out of hand she would let them know, watching from her bed and getting up if she needed to "discipline" a pup or group of pups and then quietly going back to bed. I lost Izabel in September 2013; she had inoperable cancer and passed at home in her sleep. I still think I hear her tiptoe through the house sometimes or feel her snuggling under the covers next to me. I miss her every day.

UKC/PTCA Ch Anglo-American's Ty Parks is another special Patterdale. I had Izabel for about two years when I got a call from her breeder 3 days before Christmas 2006. He had been having a horrible time and had to re-home 8 Patterdale Terriers that day or they would be going to the shelter. I called my husband and told him to go get all of our empty crates together and we went and picked up 8 mean little terriers. The dogs had no socialization, none of them got along with each other and they did not like being put in crates into our car. There was only one male in the bunch, and his name was Tyreece. He growled every time I even breathed. I only offered him food by hand, he didn't eat for two days. I had to back up and let him jump out to take him to the bathroom, but I knew since he never actually bit me I could win him over. He had been passed around a lot and had spent most of his life on a chain and would escape whenever he could and attack whatever wildlife crossed his path (including cats). That is how I got him. We had a small pet store at this time and I kept breeder rats. About a week after I got him he broke out of his cage one night and killed all of my breeder rats. When I came in the next morning he was so proud of himself he was jumping all over for approval. Even though I was furious at the little brat, I couldn't help but admire him. He knew what he was bred to do and he was so proud of his work. Almost from this moment, me and "Pieces" as I called him were never apart again. I had just lost Bizzy and missed the bond we had and Tyreece had never had that connection before and became a very willing partner and member of the family. He amazed me; I took him to his first trial a few months after I got him to see if he would have any interest in any events. Pieces was almost 5 when I got him and I had no idea if he would. Not only did he have interest but he won the under racing championship, under go-to-ground champion and placed in everything else. When we lure coursed him the first time he ran the entire track and at the end jumped in the lap of a friend's mother and rolled over for a belly rub. He was always willing to give it his all and he was even more willing to accept praise and a belly rub. He was a clown and definitely a dog I still tear up at the mention of. Pieces became my shadow, when I showered he pulled my clothes to the corner of the shower and waited for me. He went to bed when I went to bed; he got up when I got up and so on. We competed and I loved "Pieces" for just 22 months. One morning he didn't get up when I got up and I knew something was wrong. I went and got him out of bed and I realized he was not himself, he got worse over the next few days and we took him into the vet where we learned he had advanced heart damage. Although he had tested negative for heartworms when we got him he had evidence he had them at some point in his life and they had done major damage. There were options for keeping him comfortable but it was heartbreaking watching him suffer through his days and we made the decision to put him to sleep. He was truly "THE HEART DOG" and if I could clone any Patterdale it would be him.

Last but not least is: BIMBS UKC GRCH/ PTCA National Veteran Champion Anglo-American's What A Shamus Hall Of Fame, COG, and Total Dog. Shamus was the only Patterdale I ever purchased. David Mason of Tennessee bred him. Shamus is a fantastic, fun, racing machine. He is the foundation male for my line and is seen in many of the top kennels today. Shamus will be 12 this year (2014) and even though he is slower and gray these days I still see that little chocolate fur ball I picked up in Tennessee. I still see his spark when he hears a lure machine or a racing box drop or when we turn on the hose, who is the only enemy he has. Shamus is the best producing male I have owned. He produces fantastic conformation, temperaments and athleticism. He has produced many top terriers and is the grandsire to many more. He is the sire to UKC GRCH/PTCA CH UFCH USCH Fox Briar's Rebel, USR UFR UWP GRCH CMC's Heavy Metal, GRCH CMC's Shamus Reflection of MA and has several BIMBS winning sons and daughters. The cross with our lines of the Vetzel dogs to Shamus and the breeding of the best of those crosses is the recognizable Anglo-American line we have today.

What is your advice to anyone considering bringing home a Patterdale Terrier?
The main thing I try to tell people about the Patterdale is that even though they are small and do enjoy snuggling it does not mean they will be happy doing only that. Patterdales must be mentally stimulated and must have the ability to burn off their energy. I have seen many Patterdales develop behavior issues from destruction to aggression when they are not able to properly burn their energy. The nice thing about that is that they are eager to please and so they are open to such a wide variety of activities from, swimming, to running, to hunting they can fit a wide variety of active people's lifestyles.

What is your guidance to people when choosing a breeder to work with?
The best thing I can say is take your time, do your research and find a breeder who breeds dogs for the needs that you want. If you want to hunt your dog find a breeder who breeds for that. The same is true if you plan to show your dog. Breeders should know the personalities, both bad and good, of each dog they own and determine if a terrier is right for a particular owner. Breeders should be willing to be open and answer any questions you may have before AND after you purchase your terriers. I am always open to help my owners with any problem or question they have any time. I also contract first right of refusal on all my placements. If you are going to make the decision to breed a dog you should be willing to be responsible for its well-being for the rest of its life. I personally feel breeding should have a "purpose": a breeder should be able to tell you why they chose that pairing. Remember that just because a breeder is "well known" does not make them good and just because a breeder is "unknown"

does not mean they are bad. Breeders should be willing to invite you to meet their dogs and always be weary of a breeder who is unwilling to allow you to meet your puppy or its parents prior to purchasing.

Thank you, Andrea, for sharing your story. Your passion for the Patterdale Terrier is an inspiration to us all.

Figure 74: James Hoffman holds "Mighty", shown here successfully
capturing a rat on the streets of metropolitan New York, USA.
Photograph taken by William L. Reyna Jr. and used
with permission by James Hoffman.

[15]

James Hoffman

WE FIRST REACHED OUT to James Hoffman because of a New York Times article we read on November 21, 2013. The article discussed a group of terrier enthusiasts known as the Ryders Alley Trencher-fed Society (R.A.T.S.) working their dogs in the Manhattan alleyways of New York City. This group regularly meets and harnesses their dogs' strong work ethic doing their small part to help with the city's rat infestation. James and his Patterdale Terrier Mighty were called out specifically in the article. It's refreshing to see an owner providing a Patterdale the work he needs even when they reside in an urban setting.

Having the opportunity to talk with James, we quickly realized how passionate he is about dogs. He works as a veterinary technician in the city and has the soul of a terrier man. James was kind enough to share his story, which is reprinted below.

CITY SMART – COUNTRY HEART

In 2010 I set out to find a dog. I grew up hunting upland game with Brittanys and Beagles, but now live in the city and have a young family and a more than full time job as a veterinary technician. I needed a dog that could play an active role as a family pet and daily companion as well as a hunting partner. The available space of city living dictated that I have a single dog that could fill all these roles. All in all, I seem to share the terrier temperament.

After a lot of research and advice from friends, I settled on a Patterdale Terrier. The reputation of the breed as a hunter both above and below ground is legendary and I was hopeful that we could instill the "family pet qualities" as he grew. I purchased a puppy of Booth bloodlines from a breeder in California. "Diggin Deep C-4" as he is officially named, "Mighty" made the non-stop airline trip in fine style and was soon a member of our family. His first assignments were as a lap dog for my wife, a doll for my 7-year old daughter and a "rough house" pal for my 10-year old son.

From Mighty's point of view, hunting is the easy part, although finding opportunities in the city isn't always easy. He entered easily to quarry that we encountered on our nightly walks and he actively hunts raccoon, opossum and groundhog that we encounter in out of the way places. To say he is fearless is perhaps an understatement.

Over a year ago, we joined forces with a group that promotes working terriers and Dachshunds in metropolitan New York area. Hunts are held often and, in time-honored custom, consist of a "scratch pack" of terriers. Borders, Cairns, Norfolk, Bedlingtons, Jack Russells, Manchesters and Dachshunds all have an opportunity to play their part. Mighty fits seamlessly into this group and quickly developed his expertise as a catch dog, quickly snapping up rats that had been flushed by the shorter legged members of the team. His manners in the field with the other dogs are impeccable. Like any good terrier, Mighty can change instantly from a family pet to a very effective hunting machine.

To be sure, the Patterdale temperament requires a constructive outlet and being part of the Ryder's Alley Trencher-fed Society (R.A.T.S.) provides that outlet. Mighty has received a lot of notoriety both across the United States and as far away as France, Germany and England where he has been featured in print, on video and even reality TV. His instinctive hunting ability and acquired team training have made him an excellent ambassador for Patterdales everywhere.

Befitting his instinctive hunting ability, Mighty earned a Certificate of Gameness from the American Working Terrier Association on his first attempt. He will be aiming at a Working Certificate from the AWTA.

Now a bit more than three years old, Mighty is nearing the top of his game. He is still learning his hunting skills and we expect to have ample opportunity for den work in the countryside this summer. Meanwhile, the never-ending supply of rats in Manhattan assures all the R.A.T.S. dogs of continued opportunity.

Figure 75: "Mighty", doing his best to find the rat.
Photograph used with permission by James Hoffman.

We hope that Mighty's ability as a hunter and his adaptability as a family pet and goodwill ambassador at our veterinary practice will introduce more people to this wonderful and relatively unspoiled breed. Patterdales are not the breed for everyone and probably do best when they have a committed owner and a regular job, but for Mighty and me, we've got the ideal situation.

Figure 76: Robert Booth, photograph used with permission.

[16]

Robert Booth

ALWAYS WILLING TO SHARE his advice and stories of great men and dogs is Robert Booth. A die-hard terrier man, Robert has been working and breeding Patterdale Terriers since the early days of the breed's inception in England. He actually learned and worked with the likes of Cyril Breay, Frank Buck, and Brian Nuttall. Robert Booth also penned a book entitled, *He's Out Dogging: A Countryman's Pursuits with Lurchers and Terriers* (Booth, 1990). Robert is very active and generous with his time to those who choose to come to him for advice.

PATTERDALE PURIST

When did you first get involved with dogs?

I got deeply involved with dogs with my uncle Rodney Burgess of Congleton, Cheshire. I was almost his adopted son (*laugh*). He would take me foxing and badger digging with his terriers and lurchers. He kept about a dozen dogs but his terriers were Jack Russells.

How did you get involved with Patterdales and how long you've been working with this type?

I changed more to Patterdales as there were a few local guys who I hunted with that kept these dogs: a much younger Brian Nuttall and Frank Buck and the greatest in my opinion, old Mr. Cyril Breay. Further north, everyone always treated him with respect and called him Mr. Breay. Anyway I loved the way they worked and bred so consistent unlike many Russells, that could be more hit and miss. Though I will say, "A good terrier is a good terrier whatever the breed".

215

Wow, so you hunted with Brian Nuttall, Frank Buck, and Cyril Breay? What did you guys hunt primarily and where did you do your hunting?

No, I visited Mr. Breay and listened to him and his breeding methods but he was very old at the time and I was very young. I knew him through my uncle.

I bought a working terrier from Frank Buck that won one of the biggest national working terrier championships in the country. I got rid of him because he was just a good fox dog but not good enough on badger; which is the real acid test for any terrier.

I hunted a few times with Brian but we disagreed a few to many times (*laugh*).

Interesting, you discussed breeding methods with Mr. Breay when you were young. What was some of the advice he passed along? What were the rules he followed in his breeding program?

His rule of thumb was "twice in and once out, before going back in, but never be kennel blind and try to improve or correct faults in your line with every outcross."

What rules do you follow in your breeding program?

I've always done something similar; but if a particular breeding works well with 100% of the produce, I try and repeat it or as close as I can, nothing that clever really.

Do you only breed animals that have shown to be good workers in the field?

Yes, but I have had well-bred young untried ones have had an accidental mating and throw great workers. "An ounce of breeding is worth a ton of feeding" my old uncle used to say. He also said, "It costs as much to keep a good one as a bad one, so why keep a bad one".

What is your definition of a "Good One"?

A "Good One" is first and foremost, a great finder with a great nose. I will not keep any dog or bitch that does not stick at its quarry until dug to, whether that it is just a couple of hours or even when it runs into days in extreme cases.

Any great dogs that you have come across that have a story you can share?

One Saturday morning I turned my Bruiser dog into what I thought was a handy badger set, only to discover it joined to air vents and mine shafts. It was Monday afternoon before we eventually got to him. He was still doing his job very exhausted and at a point of collapse but locked solid onto the nose of a badger. Dog and quarry were dug successfully some 56 hours after he entered. I also had a very similar experience with his great grandfather my old Sam dog some 20 years earlier.

Wow, impressive. Would you have any advice for someone who is interested in getting started hunting with Patterdales?

If you go to buy a puppy, buy from proven parents that throw workers from lines that often click well together. When you view the pups take a little fur on a string or cane. If the puppies are not interested don't buy one. Not a guarantee but a useful guideline.

Anything else you would like to share (good Patterdale books, advice on healthcare, or anything else on you mind)?

I think the book *The Fell Terrier by Brian Plumber* is probably the best Patterdale book ever written as each chapter was more or less the words of England's best old time terrier men.

Couldn't agree more on Brian's book. It's a great resource and unfortunate that it's out of print. Thank you, Robert, for sharing your experiences of hunting with your Patterdales.

Bibliography

Black, R. (2011). *Hunting Songs Volume One: The Lakeland Fell Packs*. Windsor-Spice Books.

Bloeme, P. (1994). *Frisbee Dogs: How to Raise, Train and Compete*. Atlanta: Prb & Assoc.

Booth, R. (1990). *He's Out Dogging: A Countryman's Pursuits with Lurchers and Terriers*. Booth Fieldsports Publications.

Burns, P. (2005). *American Working Terriers*. Raleigh, NC: Lulu.com.

Dunbar, D. I. (2004). *Before & After Getting Your Puppy*. Novato, CA, USA: New World Library.

Frain, S. (2004). *The Patterdale Terrier*. Wykey, Shrewsbury, UK: Swan Hill Press.

Plummer, D. B. (1998). *The Fell Terrier*. Machynlleth, Powys, UK: Coch-y-Bonddu Books.

Volhard, J. a. (2010). *Dog Training For Dummies*. Hoboken, NJ: Wiley Publishing, Inc.

Index

ABOUT THE AUTHORS

Figure 77: Photograph used with permission by Chris Meagh.

Michael, Jennifer and their daughter Skylar are active Patterdale Terrier enthusiasts. They keep their home base in Atlanta, GA but travel throughout the Southeastern United States attending terrier events. Skylar is a regular fixture in UKC, PTCA, and JRTCA shows and has enjoyed junior handling since she was five years old. Jennifer earned her Bachelor of Arts in Art History from the University of Georgia. Jennifer is a founding member of the Earth Works Terrier Association and is an officer in the Dogwood Jack Russell Terrier Club. She contributes her creative talents to their web presence and public relations. Michael has been a dog devotee and trainer since he was a child. He received his Bachelor of Science in Molecular Biology from the Georgia Institute of Technology and went on to receive his Master of Science from Georgia State University. Before becoming an avid terrierman, Michael was a competitor in national Frisbee dog competitions and was an active member of the Greater Atlanta Dog and Disc Club. The Millers share their home and lives with two high-spirited Patterdale Terriers and two tolerant rescue dogs.

CPSIA information can be obtained at www.ICGtesting.com
Printed in the USA
BVOW07*1825061115

426102BV00002B/2/P

9 780989 865203